VISUO-SPATIAL
WORKING MEMORY

Visuo-Spatial Working Memory

Robert H. Logie

Department of Psychology
University of Aberdeen
Aberdeen, UK

 LAWRENCE ERLBAUM ASSOCIATES, PUBLISHERS
Hove (UK)   Hillsdale (USA)

Lawrence Erlbaum Associates Ltd., Publishers
27 Palmeira Mansions
Church Road
Hove
East Sussex, BN3 2FA
UK

British Library Cataloguing in Publication Data

A catalogue record for this book is available from the British Library

ISBN 0-86377-107-6
ISSN 0959-4779

Printed and bound by BPC Wheatons Ltd., Exeter

For Elizabeth

Contents

Acknowledgements

The production of this essay was greatly assisted by a goodly number of people who offered support and productive discussion. I should particularly like to mention the numerous and stimulating dialogues with my friends and colleagues, Alan Baddeley, Sergio Della Sala, Ken Gilhooly, Marc Marschark, and Dan Reisberg. I am also grateful to Sergio Della Sala and to Marc Marschark for making it possible for me to have brief sabbaticals respectively in Northern Italy and in North Carolina. Those visits and my discussions with Sergio and with Marc gave significant impetus to ideas in this book. I should also like to express my thanks both to Gerry Quinn and to Maria Brandimonte for helpful, supportive, and insightful comments on an earlier draft of the manuscript. Finally, I am grateful for the indulgence and support of my wife Elizabeth and my sons Matthew and Andrew, and for their tolerance of the single-mindedness and preoccupation that accompanies scientific scribing.

Preface

Representation of the visual and spatial properties of our environment is a pivotal requirement of everyday cognition. We can mentally represent the visual form of objects. We can extract information from several of the senses as to the location of objects in relation to ourselves and to other objects nearby. We can reach out and manipulate some of those objects. We can also imagine ourselves manipulating objects in advance of doing so, or even when it would be impossible to do so physically. The problem posed to science is how these cognitive operations are accomplished, and proffered accounts lie in two essentially parallel research endeavours: working memory and imagery. Working memory is thought to pervade everyday cognition, to provide on-line processing and temporary storage, and to update, moment-to-moment, our representation of the current state of our environment and our interactions with that environment. There is now a strong case for the claims of working memory in the area of phonological and articulatory functions, all of which appear to contribute to everyday activities such as counting, arithmetic, vocabulary acquisition, and some aspects of reading and language comprehension. The claims for visual and spatial working memory functions are less convincing. Most notable has been the assumption that visual and spatial working memory are intimately involved in the generation, retention, and manipulation of visual images. Until recently, there has been little hard evidence to justify that assumption, and the research on visual and spatial working memory has focused on a relatively restricted range of imagery tasks and phenomena. In a more or less independent development the literature on visual imagery has now amassed a voluminous corpus of data and theory about a wide range of imagery phenomena, but sadly little of the imagery literature refers to the concept of working memory. This essay follows a line of reconciliation and positive critiquing rather than adversity in attempting to test the assumptions of working memory in the visual and spatial domain.

CHAPTER ONE

Temporary Memory

FINDING YOUR WAY IN THE DARK

Suppose you were to close your eyes for a moment and attempt to describe the scene in front of you. If the scene is familiar, this may be a fairly trivial task. If the scene is new to you, the task is still possible, but it is less easy to fill in details that you may have forgotten from your most recent memory of the scene. Perhaps a more difficult task might be to ask you to navigate your way blindfold through a room that is cluttered with furniture and of which you have had only the briefest of glimpses a few moments before.

For most people these tasks would appear to involve some form of visual memory of the scene or room. What kind of memory system might be involved? Retention of the information is required over periods of seconds or minutes, thus we can discount any form of memory system such as iconic memory that is purported to retain information only for much shorter periods (e.g. Kikuchi, 1987; Purdy & Olmstead, 1984; Sperling, 1960). Similarly, the information is unlikely all to be held in some form of longer-term memory, although details about the nature of the objects in the scene could be retrieved from a long-term knowledge base. Moreover, retention of the particular form, colour, and location in the scene would more likely rely on a temporary memory trace. Also it seems reasonable to assume that much of the information in the temporary memory trace will be in a form that represents the visual and spatial properties of the scene, or at least in a form that would allow these properties to be reconstructed. It is

1

possible to use verbal labels such as "there is a bed on the left", but it is unlikely that you would have done this for all of the items in the room on the basis of a brief single viewing.

There is no doubt that most of us could perform this kind of task with some individual variability in performance. We could also carry out many other tasks that require temporary storage of visual and/or spatial information. This in turn suggests that we have some form of memory system for storing the necessary information. However, this conclusion begs a number of questions. If such a memory system is available, is it specialised for dealing with visual and/or spatial material, or could a general purpose temporary storage system suffice? If it is a specialised system, can it deal with visual and spatial information, or is the system fractionated further into two systems, one for visual and one for spatial information? Why would there be a need for a specialised system of this kind and what are the everyday tasks in which it would be involved? What determines its capacity limitations, and what sort of time limit can be described as temporary?

Much of the discussion in this book will centre around these questions, and will be based on three assertions. The first of these assertions is that the system comprises a memory function that provides storage, in some form, of visual and/or spatial information on a temporary basis. This memory system is separate from some form of more permanent memory, but information flows between the permanent and the temporary systems in the absence of sensory input. This assertion is possibly the best supported empirically, and is possibly the least controversial.

The second assertion is somewhat less widely accepted, and claims that visual and spatial working memory are best thought of as separate cognitive functions. In this conception, visual working memory is passive and contains information about static visual patterns. The system is closely linked with, but is distinct from visual perception. Elsewhere, this cognitive function has been referred to as the "inner eye" (Reisberg & Logie, 1993) or as part of the visuo-spatial scratch pad (Baddeley, 1986; Logie, 1986, 1989). A similar cognitive function has been attributed to a cognitive structure referred to as the "visual buffer" (Kosslyn, 1980). As I shall argue later, Kosslyn's visual buffer is a rather different concept, and the visuo-spatial scratch pad is seen as one system rather than two. Also, on reflection, the term "inner eye" has the trappings of an homunculus and begs questions about inner screens and the possibility of an infinite series of inner eyes watching inner screens. For these reasons, I shall adopt the term "visual cache", to distinguish the system from its predecessors and from its theoretical *doppelgängers*. In this two-component model, spatial working memory retains dynamic information about movement and movement sequences, and is linked with the control of physical actions.

Here, as elsewhere (Reisberg & Logie, 1993), I shall refer to this system as the "inner scribe". The scribe provides a means of "redrawing" the contents of the visual cache, offering a service of visual and spatial rehearsal, manipulation, and transformation.

The third assertion also flirts with polemics by maintaining that information from sensory input does not access the visual cache and the inner scribe directly but only via some form of long-term memory representation. I shall argue that this last feature is not just characteristic of the visual cache and the inner scribe, but is true generally of all of working memory. This contrasts with the traditional view that information from sensory input has to pass through working memory in transit to long-term storage. In the course of the book it should become clear that this cannot be the case, and that sensory input accesses long-term memory representations first. These representations are activated, and *ipso facto* the activated representations become available to working memory which holds the information momentarily and implements on-line processing. The information may then return to long-term memory, thereby strengthening the originating, activated trace. Alternatively, processing in working memory may generate novel information which then allows novel traces and novel associations to be stored on a more enduring basis.

In making these assertions explicit, I do not intend them to be accepted without discussion or debate, but rather to act as a focus for such debate. The intention is to investigate whether these assertions are tenable, and thereby to illuminate visuo-spatial short-term memory function, and its place within the bailiwick of working memory.

A BRIEF GUIDE

In the remainder of this chapter the investigation will proceed with a discussion of the case for a short-term memory system. In Chapter 2, I shall discuss the literature on visual imagery as a form of mental representation, and Chapter 3 will examine the range of tasks in which a visuo-spatial working memory system might be involved. Chapter 4 gives a detailed account of the working memory model on which many of the ideas in this book are based, and argues the case for separate visual and spatial elements of that model. Chapter 5 considers the range of evidence for visual and spatial working memory from patients with various forms of brain damage. The final chapter moves towards a coherent account of the evidence presented, considers ways in which the visual imagery literature and the working memory literature might have a common interest, and adds a few theoretical speculations of my own.

There is of course one important assumption underlying the rationale for this kind of book; that is whether there is indeed a strong case for *any* form of memory function that deals with information solely on a temporary basis. This topic could fill a volume on its own, and is discussed in some detail in contemporary textbooks (e.g. Baddeley, 1990; Eysenck & Keane, 1990). However it is worth considering briefly in the remainder of this chapter before going on to ask whether there is a *visuo-spatial* temporary memory system.

IS THERE A TEMPORARY STORAGE FUNCTION?

Drawing from our intuition, the ability to retain information over a short period of time seems fundamental to a wide range of tasks in everyday life. In order to know what we are going to do next we need to remember what we have just done. While counting, we have to remember how far we have gone through the counting sequence in order to know which number comes next. In reading, we have to remember what we have just read in order to make sense of what we are now reading; and we have to retain an unfamiliar telephone number just long enough to press the buttons in the right sequence. The cognitive abilities and systems that allow us to perform these tasks have a different role, and are of a different nature from memory functions that allow us to access our store of general knowledge of the world or to retrieve information about past experiences and life events. This distinction was recognised by the British philosopher John Locke as long ago as 1690.

> The next faculty of mind ... is that which I call *retention* ... This is done in two ways.
>
> First by keeping the idea which is brought into it, for some time actually in view, which is called *contemplation*.
>
> The other way of retention is, the power to revive again in our minds those ideas which, after imprinting have disappeared, or have been as it were laid aside out of sight ... This is *memory* which is as it were the storehouse of our ideas. (Locke, 1690, Book II, Chapter X, paragraphs 1–2)

There has been considerable effort directed towards understanding how human temporary storage of information is achieved. The prevailing view during the 1950s was that memory was a single system, that there was no distinction between temporary storage and longer-term storage, and that the same system was involved in retaining a telephone number and recalling lengthy sequences of prose learned at school. In addition the prevailing experimental techniques of the time involved presentation and retrieval of lists of verbal material rather than aspects of everyday cognition.

In 1965 an influential paper by Waugh and Norman revived an idea similar to the Locke distinction, which had been proposed by William James in 1890. Their suggestion was of two memory systems: a primary memory, responsible for short-term storage and a secondary memory responsible for longer-term storage. Information in primary memory was thought to be displaced by new material unless it was maintained by rehearsal. Information could be copied from primary memory to secondary memory by means of rehearsal.

Recency and Short-term Memory

One of the major sources of evidence for a distinction between primary and secondary memory came from experiments involving short-term retention of word lists. In this sort of experiment subjects are presented with a list of items, and are then asked to recall as many of the items as they can in any order (known as free recall). What tends to happen in this situation is that people start by recalling the last few items in the list, and this they can do very well. Next they will recall the first few list items, and performance here is again reasonably good. Finally they will attempt to recall as many items as they can from the middle positions in the list. The tendency to recall accurately items from the end of the list is known as the recency effect because these are the most recently presented items in the list. The tendency to do reasonably well at the beginning of the list is known as the primacy effect. The overall pattern is referred to as the serial position curve (Glanzer & Cunitz, 1966; First reported by Nipher, 1876).

Figure 1.1 shows the serial position curve derived from free recall by a sample of 30 subjects, of 10 lists of 12 bisyllabic words (Capitani, Della Sala, Logie, & Spinnler, 1992). This is the pattern when recall occurs immediately after the list has been presented. However if there is a filled delay of even a few seconds (during which the subject performs a simple, unrelated task) before recall is required, then the primacy effect is retained but the recency effect disappears. After a delay the last few list items are remembered no better than items from the middle of the list.

The effect of a delay on recency but not primacy was taken by a number of authors to suggest that primacy reflected a long-term or secondary memory system while recency reflected the operation of a short-term or primary memory system. It was thought that items early in the list would be rehearsed and would therefore enter long-term memory. Rehearsal would be more difficult as the number of items in the list increased, and therefore transfer to long-term memory would be much less efficient. Items near the end of the list would still be in a short-term store immediately after list presentation, but would be displaced by other material after a delay. There are a large number of papers on this topic, but a typical study

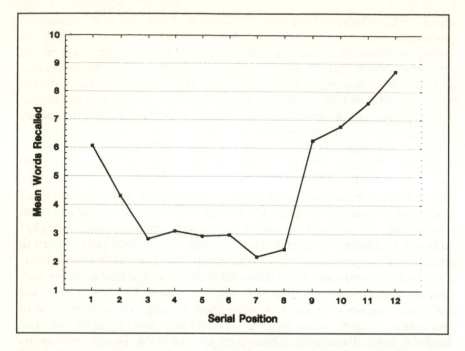

FIG. 1.1. Serial position curve derived from free recall by a sample of 30 normal subjects, of 10 lists of 12 bisyllabic words (Capitani, Della Sala, Logie, & Spinnler, 1992).

is reported by Glanzer and Cunitz (1966). Although initially these data seemed to provide very strong evidence for a distinction between two memory systems, subsequent work has indicated that the recency effect may not after all uniquely reflect the operation of a short-term store (for reviews see Capitani et al, 1992; Greene, 1986).

One difficulty with the short-term memory interpretation of recency arose from the report by Baddeley and Hitch (1977) that free recall of the details of rugby matches taking place over a period of several months showed the familiar serial position curve, with events early in the sporting season showing a primacy effect, and events taking place over the few weeks prior to memory test showing a recency effect. It is clear that recency spread over several weeks could not reflect the operation of a short-term memory system. A second difficulty was reported by Watkins and Peynircioglu (1983), where subjects were given lists of 45 items, but with the items from three different categories (riddles, objects, and sounds). When recall was tested subjects showed three separate recency effects for each of the three categories of items even although they had been presented mixed in a single list. These findings suggested that recency was a phenomenon of long-term storage as well as a phenomenon of immediate free recall.

Neuropsychology also contributed to the demise of recency as a phenomenon specifically of short-term memory. A number of demented patients have been reported who had severely impaired verbal memory span[1] (a standard test of short-term memory capacity), but appeared to show normal recency (Spinnler & Della Sala, 1988; Wilson, Bacon, Fox, & Kaszniak, 1983). In normal adults (Martin, 1978) and in patient populations (Della Sala, Pasetti, & Sempio, 1987) that show normal recency and span there are very poor correlations between span and measures of recency. Hitch and Halliday (1983) have shown that recency and memory span appear to develop at different rates in young children, further supporting the idea of a dissociation between these two phenomena. In addition, memory span is invariably impaired by concurrent articulation of an irrelevant word, a technique referred to as articulatory suppression (e.g. Baddeley, Thomson, & Buchanan, 1975; Levy, 1971; Murray, 1968). However, recency is unaffected by concurrent articulation (Richardson & Baddeley, 1975).

Further evidence that undermined the link between recency and short-term memory arose from the use of the continuous distractor paradigm. This involves interspersing the presentation of each item with some distractor activity throughout the list (Bjork & Whitten, 1974; Tzeng, 1973). The last item is also followed by this distractor activity, but under these conditions both primacy and recency appear very clearly, whereas if the distracter appears only after the last item and not throughout the list, the usual disruption of recency appears. This adds to the doubt as to whether recency genuinely reflects the functioning of a short-term memory system.

There are currently two alternative explanations for the recency effect: one that it reflects a retrieval strategy (Baddeley & Hitch, 1977; Baddeley, 1986), and the other that it reflects temporal discrimination of memory traces (e.g. Crowder, 1976; Glenberg et al., 1980). Crowder describes this last interpretation in terms of watching telephone poles receding into the distance. Those that are close can be discriminated easily, and those that are more distant merge together and are more difficult to discriminate from one another. So too with memory traces receding in time. Those traces that are recent are more readily discriminated than those more distant in time.

These explanations are not necessarily mutually exclusive, in that a sensible retrieval strategy would be to recall those items that are most readily discriminable, rather than, say, recalling items in their original order of presentation. This provides an arguable case for recency being a general phenomenon of memory, applying both to short-term and to long-term memory. Thus the recency effect is still considered by many authors to be associated with a short-term memory function, although not uniquely so.

A more recent view of verbal short-term memory is that it comprises more than one component, specifically a passive, phonological store and an articulatory rehearsal process (see later discussion and Chapter 4). According to this approach, measures of memory span may reflect the operation of one component of verbal short-term memory (articulatory rehearsal), while recency reflects the other component of short-term memory (the phonological store). This view would account for the lack of association between these two measures of short-term memory performance (Vallar & Papagno, 1986). Because articulatory suppression is thought to disrupt articulatory rehearsal, this account would also cope with the resistance of recency to this form of suppression. However recency is not only resistant to the effects of articulatory suppression, it is also resistant to techniques that are thought (Salamé & Baddeley, 1982; 1989) to disrupt the contents of the phonological store, such as irrelevant speech played to the subjects throughout presentation of the word lists for recall (Logie, Trivelli, & Della Sala, 1993).

This essay is not the most appropriate venue for a detailed discussion of recency in verbal short-term storage, and more detailed discussions are given in Della Sala and Logie (1993) and Capitani et al. (1992). Suffice it to say that verbal recency is a robust phenomenon which has yet to be fully explained. It does nonetheless seem to be telling us something about the nature of temporary memory function and as such is worth exploring in the visuo-spatial memory domain. As is clear from the discussion so far, the vast majority of the studies on recency have focused on verbal recall tasks. However, a number of authors have reported recency effects in visual short-term memory (e.g. Broadbent & Broadbent, 1981; Phillips & Christie, 1977a). Moreover, some current thinking on recency is moving towards the suggestion that it reflects the temporary activation of long-term memory traces, and that working memory may be involved only in the retrieval of those traces (Baddeley & Hitch, 1993; Logie, Trivelli, & Della Sala, 1993). This view has implications for a model of working memory which is accessed by sensory input only indirectly via the activation of long-term memory traces. It is for these reasons that I have dwelt on the discussion of the recency effect. I shall return to this topic when discussing visual recency effects in Chapter 3, and when the "indirect" route to working memory is fleshed out in subsequent chapters (see also Logie, in press).

Memory Codes and Memory Systems

Short-term and long-term storage also have been dissociated through differences in the nature of memory coding. Conrad in 1964 demonstrated that when subjects are asked to retain a sequence of letters in order, memory performance is poorer when the letters sound very similar to one another. Thus a sequence such as D,C,B,T,P,V is rather more difficult to retain than is a sequence such as L,W,K,F,R,T. This acoustic similarity effect disrupts the order of recall of the letters for short-term serial recall. In 1966, Baddeley (Baddeley, 1966a; 1966b) contrasted recall of short sequences of acoustically similar words such as "mad map man" and acoustically dissimilar words such as "bus clock spoon", with recall of short sequences of semantically similar words such as "huge big great". He found that with short-term recall, the sets of acoustically similar words were less well recalled than were acoustically dissimilar words. However, the semantically similar words resulted in recall performance that was very little different from recall of semantically distinct words. In contrast, after a delay the effect of acoustic similarity disappeared but an effect of semantic similarity was evident, with semantically similar words recalled less well than semantically distinct words. As acoustic similarity appeared to affect short-term storage and semantic similarity appeared to affect long-term storage, this suggested that a short-term storage system retains words in terms of their sounds while the longer-term system retains words in terms of their meaning.

This distinction between the effects of different forms of similarity still holds. However the conclusions about coding differences is somewhat complicated by the fact that semantic information does appear to influence short-term storage. For example, Wetherick (1975) showed that words which were drawn from semantic groupings were recalled better in immediate memory tasks than were words not so arranged. Hulme, Maughan, and Brown (1991) have shown that memory span for words is higher than is memory span for non-words. (See also La Pointe & Engle, 1990; Shulman, 1970).

Neuropsychological Dissociations

Much stronger support for the dichotomous view of memory was provided by a number of patients with neurological damage, notably patient "H.M." described by Scoville and Milner in 1957 (see also Milner, Corkin, & Teuber, 1968; Shimamura, 1989). Following surgery for the relief of severe epilepsy, H.M. suffered bilateral damage to the temporal lobes and to the hippocampus. He had a very pronounced amnesia, with a grossly defective ability to learn new information. Despite this, H.M. showed comparatively normal intelligence, and normal ability to retain short sequences of digits. Although H.M. is the best known such patient he is not an isolated case, and a number of other such patients have been described, (e.g. Butters & Cermack, 1986; Damasio et al., 1985; Della Sala & Spinnler, 1986; Teuber, Milner, & Vaughan, 1968; Wilson & Baddeley, 1988; Zola-Morgan, Squire & Ammaral, 1986).

These amnesic patients provided evidence for damage to a long-term memory system, (strictly speaking, the damage was to long-term retention of new information, as they had less impaired access to information learned prior to the injury), but with intact short-term storage. The converse characteristics have also been found. For example, patient K.F. (Shallice & Warrington 1970; Warrington & Shallice, 1969) suffered damage to the left parieto-occipital region following a motorcycle accident. He was mildly aphasic, but had no general amnesia and long-term learning was normal. However, he could remember a sequence of only three digits and had a recency effect confined to the very last item in the list. A number of other patients have been described with similar characteristics, (e.g. Luria, Sokolov, & Kilmkowski, 1967; Shallice & Butterworth, 1977; Warrington, Logue, & Pratt, 1971). One more recent patient, P.V., has been studied in some considerable detail (e.g. Basso, Spinnler, Vallar, & Zanobio, 1982; Vallar & Baddeley, 1984; Vallar & Papagno, 1986). Caplan and Waters (1990) provide a comprehensive list of 16 short-term memory patients who have been described in the published literature.

These contrasting patterns of memory impairment in neuro-psychological patients represent the use of the powerful technique of double dissociation (Teuber, 1955) to support the fractionation of memory into two distinct systems. Note that it would not have been sufficient to show just one half of the dissociation, as this could have been attributed to a differential difficulty in the tasks performed by the patients. For example, patient H.M. had great difficulty in long-term learning, but could readily retain a sequence of digits. This pattern could be interpreted by suggesting that H.M. had a general loss of cognitive resources, and that those resources that remained could cope with the relatively simple task of retaining a set of digits over a few seconds, but could not cope with the ostensibly demanding task of laying down more permanent memory traces. Such an interpretation runs into problems when confronted by patients such as P.V. who show the reverse pattern, and the case for two memory systems is greatly strengthened. (For a comprehensive discussion of dissociation techniques and theory development see Shallice, 1988.)

PRIMARY MEMORY AS CONTROL FOR PROCESSING

Unlike the data on recency and on coding differences in normal subjects, the double dissociation found among neuropsychological patients provided very convincing support for the idea that memory was better thought of as comprising two systems, dealing respectively with short-term and with long-term memory. The Waugh and Norman model of primary and secondary memory appeared to provide a useful framework within which to encompass this two-store view of memory. However, their model had a number of limitations. Apart from the difficulty with the interpretation of the recency effect, the model dealt only with verbal rehearsal and storage. It is clear that we have available a wide variety of strategies for storing material, and verbal rehearsal is only one of these. For example it is well established that the use of visual imagery can lead to much better memory performance than does verbal rehearsal (e.g. Paivio, 1971).

In an attempt to encompass the more general notion of processes in primary memory, Atkinson and Shiffrin (1968; 1971) proposed a modification that involved a rather more complex short-term memory system, comprising limited storage space and a number of control processes. The control processes could be used to encode information in long-term memory and to maintain information in the short-term store. The short-term store was therefore seen as a working buffer rather than a passive storage system, and the control processes could include both verbal rehearsal and other coding strategies such as imagery.

However the Atkinson and Shiffrin model (sometimes referred to as the "modal model") did not fully develop the notion of the control processes, and it was unclear why some processes lead to better long-term retention than do others. One attempt to formalise this relationship was provided by Craik and Lockhart (1972) in their notion of levels of processing. The idea was to emphasise the nature of processing of information rather than memory structures. Craik and Lockhart maintained that memory traces are formed as a by-product of perceptual and attentional processes. They made a distinction between physical features of stimuli, for example brightness and shape which they classified as being subject to shallow levels of processing, and the semantic features such as meaning or associations which would involve deep levels of processing. In a typical experiment by Craik and Tulving (1975) shallow processing involved classifying letters in words as being either in upper case or lower case, while deep processing involved judging whether a presented word could fit meaningfully into an incomplete sentence. Persistence in memory was related to depth of processing, in that processing material at a deep level resulted in better recall than did processing at a shallow level. This was true even when subjects were unaware that they would later be required to recall the material (see also Hyde & Jenkins 1973). Therefore the nature of the processing was more important than an intention to learn.

The levels of processing approach has an intuitive appeal, and was greeted with some enthusiasm by those who maintained a belief in a unitary memory system (e.g. Postman, 1975). This enthusiasm was misplaced however, as Craik and Lockhart's (1972) levels of processing referred largely to the operation of secondary or long-term memory. They retained the distinction between primary and secondary memory by suggesting that subjects could maintain information at a given level of processing whether it was shallow or deep. The system that allowed such maintenance was a flexible primary memory system that could deal with different codes as required by a given level (Craik & Lockhart, 1972, p. 676). However, Craik and Lockhart did not develop this particular aspect of the levels of processing approach, preferring to concentrate on the association between processing and subsequent retention in long-term memory.

The levels of processing model had one major difficulty, namely the lack of any definition of depth that did not rely on the subsequently observed level of recall. That is, there appeared to be no adequate independent measures of depth of processing. It is not sufficient to say that those items that are retained most effectively are those that have been processed most deeply. We need some way to classify the material in advance of the memory test. One possibility is to use time for processing as a measure of depth. However this too has its problems, as even with relatively shallow processing such as verbal rehearsal, long-term retention will occur eventually (e.g. Rundus, 1971). Given these difficulties, the levels of processing approach remains intuitively attractive, but provides a less tractable theoretical framework than it initially appeared to offer.

SHORT-TERM MEMORY
AS WORKING MEMORY

The view from the levels of processing stance that primary memory could deal with a variety of different codes and processes was also a feature of the Atkinson and Shiffrin modal model. While Craik and Lockhart viewed primary memory as a phenomenon arising from maintenance of information at various levels of processing, Atkinson and Shiffrin viewed primary memory as a single, multi-purpose working buffer or temporary working memory, incorporating both storage and a variety of processing functions, and acting as a means to transfer information into long-term storage.

The last of these assumptions, which saw the single flexible system as a gateway to long-term memory, ran into some considerable difficulty when confronted by the patterns of impairment and sparing in patients with verbal short-term memory deficits, such as K.F. (Warrington & Shallice, 1969) or P.V. (Basso et al., 1982). These patients have severely impaired ability to retain more than about one or two digits in a sequence. However what was damaging to the gateway hypothesis was that these patients have apparently normal long-term learning ability. That is they were able to transfer information into long-term memory despite having a severe deficit in short-term or working memory. This could only mean that either working memory is not the gateway to long-term memory, or that working memory comprises several systems, not all of which were damaged in these patients. I shall return to this issue after discussing some additional evidence from groups of normal subjects.

A common assumption of the "single flexible resource" view of working memory is that in tasks where both storage and processing are required, then the more storage is required by a task the less of the resource will be available for processing and vice versa. Support for this characteristic of working memory has been particularly prominent in the area of language processing. For example, Daneman and Carpenter (1980; 1983) devised a task with both processing and storage components. In their task, subjects were given a series of sentences to read. In addition, they were required to remember the last word of each sentence and later to recall the sequence of words from the end of each sentence. Reading comprehension was thought to make demands on processing, whereas remembering the words placed demands on storage. Subjects who have high spans (recall four or more items) appear to have a greater capacity for comprehension than do subjects with low spans. Moreover, the working memory span measure correlates well with measures of language comprehension (see e.g. Just & Carpenter, 1992 for a review).

Further support for the non-specific "processing plus storage" characteristic of working memory derives from the finding that scores on the Daneman and Carpenter working memory span task correlate with other measures of processing and storage such as counting span (Case, Kurland, & Goldberg, 1982) that do not rely as heavily on linguistic processing. For example Baddeley, Logie, Nimmo-Smith, and Brereton (1985) asked subjects to count the number of dots in each of a series of random dot arrays. In addition subjects had to remember the total number of dots in each array and later to recall these totals in sequential order. This measure of processing and storage showed respectable correlations with the Daneman & Carpenter span measure (r=0.443), and with language comprehension (r=0.46). The variance in comprehension accounted for by the counting-span measure was entirely attributable to the correlation that this measure had with the Daneman and Carpenter span.

A similar result was reported a few years later by Turner and Engle (1989) who measured subjects' performance on the Daneman and Carpenter span task, and on a numerical processing plus storage task. The numerical processing involved asking subjects to verify an arithmetic sequence and remember a word that followed each sequence, for example:

$(4 \times 2) - 3 = 6$? TABLE
$(6 / 2) + 4 = 7$? SNOW

Subjects would then have to recall TABLE SNOW. Performance on this task correlated well with the Daneman and Carpenter span, which is consistent with the view that the processing plus storage resource is not specific to language comprehension tasks.[2]

In sum, from these various studies there seems reasonable support for a single cognitive resource which can be used for processing as well as for storage, and which is sufficiently flexible to be used at least for counting and for language comprehension.

While the idea of a single flexible system seems to work with these measures of processing and storage, it is also clear that individual differences in language comprehension are not correlated with standard measures of verbal memory span such as how many digits people can remember in a sequence (Perfetti & Goldman, 1976). Moreover, the neuropsychological patients with very severe verbal short-term memory deficits appear to have very little difficulty with most forms of language comprehension (see e.g. McCarthy & Warrington, 1990a). That is, verbal short-term memory appears to be dissociated from the temporary storage and processing involved in language comprehension. In other words, the notion that working memory is a single flexible system appears to be too simplistic.

One other important prediction from the idea of a single working memory system is that combining two activities requiring the operation of this single system would make life very difficult. For example, as digit span and Daneman and Carpenter span do not correlate, would it be possible to perform language comprehension and digit span tasks at the same time?

Some insight into this question was reported by Baddeley and Hitch (1974). In one of their experiments subjects were required to retain a sequence of digits and at the same time carry out a linguistic verification task. The verification task involved presenting a sentence that described the order of a pair of letters. A pair of letters then followed and the task was to decide whether or not the sentence was an accurate description of the letters. For example:

"A follows B - AB" is false,
whereas
"B does not follow A - BA" is true.

They found that when subjects had to retain a sequence of three digits, they could recall the digits perfectly after completing the AB task, and in turn the AB task was unaffected by the concurrent digit load. With a load of six digits, there was a small increase in the time taken to carry out the verification task, but there was no effect on accuracy. These results were taken to suggest that normal subjects can indeed carry out a storage task and a processing task simultaneously with very little mutual interference. Further they indicate that there are separate cognitive mechanisms involved, one for processing and verifying the sentences and the other for storing the digits, and that these systems can operate concurrently with only a small amount of "dual-task overhead" that showed up in response times. However an alternative view would be that a single system was involved in both processing and storage, and that the relatively modest amount of mutual interference indicated that the processing demands still left some spare resource for storage (or vice versa). Another difficulty with this study is that it involved a digit preload. In other words, subjects were given the set of digits first and they were then asked to store the digits until after the linguistic verification task had been completed. Thus at least some information about the digits could have been encoded in long-term memory before the linguistic verification task started. In this respect it is not clear whether this combination of tasks actually constituted concurrent demands on working memory.

These criticisms could be less readily levelled at a more recent study by Baddeley et al. (1986) where subjects were required to perform two demanding tasks concurrently. In this case, digit span was combined with a demanding tracking task rather than language comprehension. Subjects were first asked to undertake a digit span task performed on its own, and a tracking task performed on its own. The digit span task involved presenting sequences of digits for immediate, serial ordered, oral recall. The length of the sequences gradually increased until the subjects were no longer capable of accurately remembering the sequences. Their digit span was taken to be the sequence length just below the level at which they began to fail. The tracking task involved asking subjects to place a light sensitive pen on a white square which was displayed on a computer screen. As soon as the pen touched the square it began to move at random around the screen, and the amount of time the pen was on the white square was measured by the computer. The speed with which the square moved gradually increased until subjects could keep the pen on the target square around 60% of the time, and the speed of the square at this point was taken as a measure of each subject's maximum level of performance.

Note that both digit span and the tracking task were very demanding in that both involved pushing to the limits of performance the cognitive resources required for performing the tasks. Now if a single flexible resource is involved which is used for either tracking or for digit span, we might expect that when these two tasks are combined, subjects' performance would be severely impaired. The digit span data from this experiment are shown in Fig. 1.2a. for a group of young subjects and for a

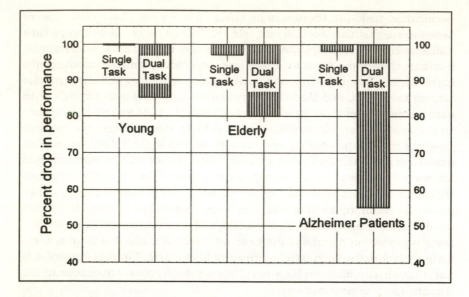

FIG. 1.2a. Digit span when performed as a single task and when coupled with concurrent tracking for groups of healthy young and healthy elderly subjects and a group of patients suffering from Alzheimer's disease.

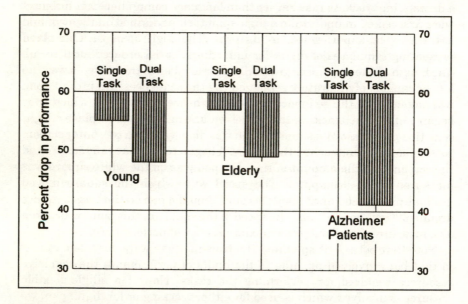

FIG. 1.2b. Tracking performance when performed alone and when performed concurrently with digit span for groups of healthy young and healthy elderly subjects and a group of patients suffering from Alzheimer's disease.

group of healthy elderly subjects. Figure 1.2b shows data for the tracking task from the same experiment. What is immediately apparent is that although there was a significant drop in performance on each task under dual task conditions, the absolute magnitude of this impairment was really rather small. The dual task effect on performance was nowhere near as devastating as might be expected if just a single system were involved in performing each of these apparently very demanding tasks.

Taken together these data make a strong case against a model that suggests that only a single, flexible, cognitive resource is involved in working memory tasks. An alternative view of working memory is that it comprises a number of components, each of which serves different functions, and only one of which matches the characteristics of the processing and storage resource referred to by Just and Carpenter (1992).

One multicomponent model of working memory that has been singularly successful in accounting for a wide range of data, including those described earlier, was proposed by Baddeley and Hitch in 1974. Baddeley and Hitch were concerned not only to account for the apparently conflicting data on short-term memory in the literature at the time, but also to consider how such a cognitive mechanism might be used outside the laboratory in everyday cognition. Their concept of working memory was as a coherent set of specialised short-term memory functions. These functions comprised a central executive that was responsible for reasoning, decision making, and for coordinating the functions of a number of specialised slave systems. Two slave systems were proposed in the original 1974 paper. One slave system, originally named the articulatory loop, was thought to be responsible for temporary retention of verbal material. Subsequently this has become known as the phonological loop (see Baddeley, 1990; 1992; Baddeley & Logie, 1992) for reasons that will be discussed in Chapter 4, and I shall tend to use the latter term. The other system, originally referred to as the visuo-spatial sketch pad, or VSSP, was thought to be responsible for temporary storage of visual and/or spatial material. This system subsequently has been referred to as the visuo-spatial scratch pad (see e.g. Baddeley, 1986), although as argued at the beginning of this chapter it may not be appropriate to think of this as a single component of working memory, and I shall use the term visuo-spatial working memory as a collective descriptor for the range of cognitive functions involved. I shall use the more specific terms visual cache and inner scribe when referring to the associated specific functions. A schematic diagram of the working memory model is shown in Fig. 1.3.

Although only two slave systems were proposed in the original model, Baddeley and Hitch recognised that there might be other slave systems with other forms of specialised functions, for example tactile, kinaesthetic, or olfactory. However, there have been few attempts to gather evidence for

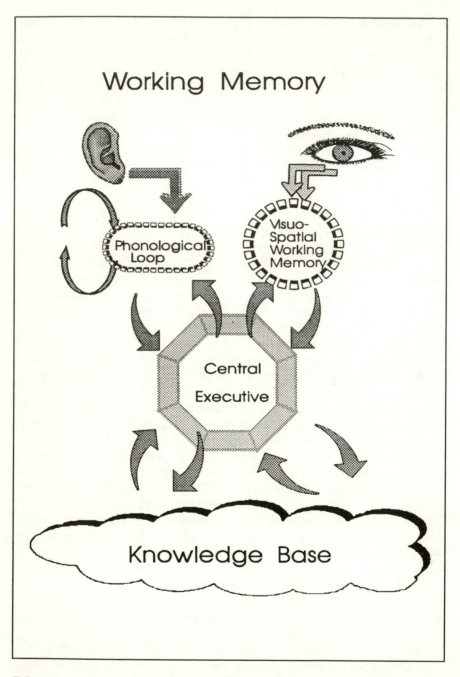

FIG. 1.3. A schematic diagram of the working memory model proposed by Baddeley (1986; Baddeley & Hitch, 1974).

such systems, and some recent work by Ellis (1991) has demonstrated that codes based on these alternative sensory modalities are very poor predictors of memory performance relative to the effects of verbal and visual codes.

The working memory model was able to account for a wide variety of data with relatively few assumptions. It was firmly set in the context of a dissociation with long-term memory, but argued that short-term memory could be usefully fractionated. The model also has gone some way to fulfilling the promise that it can account for aspects of everyday cognition (for a review see Logie, 1993). The phonological loop appears to have a role in counting and in mental arithmetic (Logie & Baddeley, 1987; Logie, Gilhooly, & Wynn, 1994), in vocabulary acquisition by young children (Gathercole & Baddeley, 1989; 1990) and by adults learning a second language (Baddeley, Papagno, & Vallar, 1988). Working memory is also thought to be involved in problem solving (Gilhooly, Logie, Wetherick, & Wynn, 1993; Johnson-Laird, 1983; Saariluoma, 1991), and in comprehension (Baddeley & Lewis, 1981; Baddeley et al., 1985; Just & Carpenter, 1992; McCarthy & Warrington, 1990a,b).

Until recently, the role of the visuo-spatial working memory (VSWM) system has been much less clear, although it was assumed to be separate from both the central executive and from the phonological loop. In subsequent studies, the characteristics of VSWM were explored in more detail, and the relevant studies will be described in later chapters.

TEMPORARY STORAGE AND PARALLEL DISTRIBUTED PROCESSING

This essay has a strong empirical emphasis. However any review of research on memory would have an ostrich-like quality if it did not consider the dramatic developments of the last decade in developing computational models of human cognition, particularly using the concept of parallel distributed processing (PDP). The suggestion is of a number of associative networks of nodes, where each node represents a unit of information, and the network is constructed by linking groups of nodes together. The links are formed through repeated association, for example between a presented stimulus and an appropriate output, analogous to the process of learning. The strength of these links vary, or have different weights, and the patterns or groupings formed through repeated associations of this kind can represent clusters of information. As a basis for a model of memory the PDP approach has a number of very attractive features: it accounts for graceful degradation in memory loss—memory function is rarely completely lost all at once for example as a result of brain disease. It therefore provides a convenient way of building computer models of learning and memory.

A full discussion of PDP approaches is well outside the scope of this volume. However one issue was notable by its absence in the major references on the topic (McClelland & Rumelhart, 1986; Rumelhart & McClelland, 1986), namely temporary storage. Networks of the kind envisaged within PDP are suited to the setting up of fairly permanent associations. Initially at least there was little consideration of just how a temporary storage function would fit into such a framework. Moreover, as the functioning of these networks is inherently parallel, this raises a particularly thorny problem when it comes to representing serial order for example in oral serial ordered recall. In more recent years this situation has begun to change, and a number of parallel distributed models of short-term memory, particularly of verbal short-term memory have been explored (Brown, 1989, 1990; Burgess & Hitch, 1992; Grossberg & Stone, 1986; Hinton & Plaut, 1987; Schneider & Detweiler, 1987; Schreter & Pfeifer, 1989; Schweickert, Guentert, & Hersberger, 1989). The problem of dealing with serial order has also been tackled for example by Brown (1989; 1990), Burgess and Hitch (1992), Houghton (1990), and Jordan (1986).

The models dealing with temporary storage have tended to be of two kinds. One type of model suggests that temporary storage relies on temporary reactivation of existing networks. The second type of model involves separate, more general purpose networks that can set up links on a temporary basis.

Hinton and Plaut (1987) proposed a model of the first type, which incorporates a distinction between fast weights and slow weights. Slow weights take some time to build up, but also take a long time to change once they are established, and are thus associated with long-term memory. Fast weights may be superimposed on slow weights, and build up very quickly but are also changed very quickly with the presentation of new stimuli to the network. The fast weights offer a way of implementing a model of short-term memory, by temporary changes in the weights of an existing network. As such, short-term memory is essentially seen as a "reactivation" of long-term memory traces. A crucial difficulty with the Hinton and Plaut (1987) concept was that their computational model was developed without adequate consideration of data derived from human experimental psychology. For example, it is not at all clear from their model how to incorporate the finding that human subjects tend to rely on a phonological code for serial ordered recall (Baddeley, 1966a; Conrad, 1964).

Schreter and Pfeifer (1989) described a model of short-term memory based on a limited number of slots for information. Their model can simulate the serial position curve in free recall, generating both primacy and recency effects. However, as argued earlier, recency can no longer be considered unequivocally and uniquely to reflect the operation of a short-term store, and the use of a slot-based model is rather simplistic.

More sophisticated models that take account of human data have been described by Schneider and Detweiler (1987), by Brown (1989; 1990), and by Burgess and Hitch (1992). What is interesting about these models is that they rely on the concept of a limited-term network of associations that is quite distinct from long-term memory representations. Indeed both Brown and Burgess and Hitch based their deliberations on the working memory model, specifically the phonological loop. Brown's model was developed as a hybrid of an existing PDP model of speech perception (Norris, 1990) and another model of speech production (Jordan, 1986). Temporal sequencing is dealt with by incorporating a decay function for activations in the network. The level of decay can be used to determine how recently a particular part of the network has been activated. This approach reflects some key features of models based on human experimental data (Baddeley, 1986; Schweickert & Boruff, 1986) and has been moderately successful in implementing a computational model of short-term verbal storage.

Burgess and Hitch (1992) use the concept of "competitive queuing" to represent recall in serial order, and this is an approach that has also been successful in modelling aspects of speech production (Brown, 1989; 1990). That is, each item is retained at a node with a given level of activation, and with weights between one node and the next in sequence. Recalling one node has the effect of suppressing that node and raising the activation of the item that follows. The process of competitive queuing involves selection for output of the node that is most active at any one time, and the model builds in an element of "noise" in the system which allows errors to occur.

What is attractive about the Burgess and Hitch model is that it generates a number of the patterns of data typically obtained from human subjects, such as the phonological similarity effect, the word length effect, and the primacy effect. (For a discussion of these effects in the human data see Chapter 4.) Their initial form of the model also had limitations in that it did not adequately simulate a number of short-term verbal memory phenomena such as the effects of articulatory suppression, or the recency effect. It is interesting that Burgess and Hitch then went on to modify their model in order that it could adequately simulate the recency effect. However the discussion on the recency effect earlier in this chapter suggests that this modification was unnecessary because the phonological loop may not be responsible for recency in any case.

An important point raised by Burgess and Hitch is that their endeavour is motivated by a desire to model human data. In contrast, other attempts to model serial order have used algorithms, simply because these algorithms can handle sequencing rather than because the algorithms might do this in a way that might illuminate how retention of serial order is accomplished by human beings. This is a key point not just for modelling of temporary memory, but because a failure to consider human data is not an uncommon feature in computer simulations of human cognition.

These latter developments suggest that the connectionist modelling of at least the phonological loop component of working memory may prove to be fruitful. At the same time it is crucial to think carefully about what motivates the development of these models, even in the cases when human data are considered. At one level it could be argued that the modelling merely confirms that it is possible to reproduce in a computer simulation some of the phenomena that have been reported in laboratory studies of human subjects. In the context of cognitive psychology, this in itself may be of little value, as it does not add much to what we know already about human cognition from the laboratory studies that gave rise to the phenomena being modelled. If in the process of modelling we are forced to ask questions as to the detailed operation of our models of cognition then this may add considerable insight. However, we should also be circumspect here in that the questions are of value only if they concern the understanding of human cognition rather than the technical limitations or vagaries of the particular modelling techniques adopted.

There have been no attempts to develop computational models, of the PDP type or otherwise, specifically of visuo-spatial working memory. Suggestions as to how this might be done may be gleaned from network models of visual perception and visual imagery (e.g. Hinton, McClelland, & Rumelhart, 1986; Kosslyn, 1991; Kosslyn, Chabris, Marsolek, & Koenig, 1992; Pinker, 1988), although as I shall argue later it is important to be clear as to where the overlaps occur between the theoretical constructs and phenomena in studies of imagery and the constructs and phenomena in studies of visual working memory (Logie, 1991). In part, the scant attention to computational modelling may reflect the extent to which VSWM is under-specified on the basis of the laboratory experiments with human participants. This is an issue I shall return to in Chapters 3 and 4 when considering models of visual imagery and visual working memory in more detail.

CONCLUDING THE CASE FOR SHORT-TERM MEMORY

The case for a separate short-term memory system is not without its critics. It is a case that I have argued in outline, as to do so in full would have been at the expense of the main topic of this book. However, the concept of a short-term memory provides an adequate explanation for a variety of memory phenomena, and for some patterns of memory impairment following neurological damage. It also appears to be a concept that can, in principle at least, be modelled in connectionist networks taking into account both computational rigour and patterns of data from human subjects. As such the case seems sufficiently strong to merit a closer look at the detailed, functional characteristics of short-term memory, and indeed whether one function of short-term memory is to store and manipulate visuo-spatial information. The case for such a view is the subject of the remaining chapters in this book.

NOTES

1.   Memory span is typically defined as the longest sequence of unrelated items (commonly digits, presented auditorily) an individual can recall correctly in an immediate serial ordered recall task. Although it is a widely used measure of short-term verbal memory capacity, it is notable that there is no universally agreed method for measuring verbal memory span. There is also a debate as to the most appropriate method for measuring recency. However the lack of a link between span and recency discussed here has been demonstrated with a range of measures of span and of recency.

2.   Turner and Engle's argument is of course based on the assumption that arithmetic processing is inherently non-linguistic. This assumption might be challenged by authors who argue that mathematical problem solving involves heavy reliance on the principles of language, for example to access vocabularies of known sums, to invoke practised algorithms for calculation, and to provide temporary storage of partial solutions (e.g. Campbell & Graham, 1985; Dehaene, 1992; Logie, Gilhooly & Wynn, 1994; McCloskey, 1992).

CHAPTER TWO

Mental Representation

The previous chapter was concerned with whether there was a sufficiently convincing case to allow us to maintain the concept of a separate temporary memory system. The conclusion was highly optimistic as to the fruitfulness of continuing to explore the concept. In this chapter I shall discuss how such a short-term memory system might be involved in dealing with visual information, whether this originates from visual perception or from long-term memory traces. Both facets of temporary visual storage should have an important role in visual imagery, and this is an area where there has been considerable research activity over the last two decades. In particular the overlap in the cognitive resources required for visual imagery and for visual perception has been explored extensively. I do not intend to provide here a comprehensive review of work on visual imagery, as there are already excellent reviews published elsewhere (e.g. Denis, 1989; Finke, 1989). However any self-respecting visual short-term memory system ought to play a key role in generating and retaining visual images, and it is important to set this role in the context of what is now a large literature. This chapter will present an overview of the main findings in this literature that are germane to the topic of the book.

MENTAL ROTATION

Our ability to transform mental images, for example by rotation, is now well established, although there remains a debate as to how exactly mental transformations take place (e.g. Kosslyn, 1980; Pylyshyn, 1973, 1981;

Shepard & Cooper, 1982). The seminal work on this topic was carried out by Shepard and Metzler (1971), where they presented subjects with pictures showing perspective views of pairs of three-dimensional objects (see Fig. 2.1.). The second item of the pair could be a rotated version of the first item, or a rotated version of a mirror image of the first item. The subjects' task was to determine whether the items in each pair depicted two identical objects, or depicted an enantiomorphic (mirror-reversed) pair.

Shepard and Metzler found that the time to make a decision was linearly related to the difference in the angle of orientation of the two depicted objects. This was true whether the rotation was in the two-dimensional plane of the picture, or was in three-dimensional perspective. This kind of result has been replicated many times with two-dimensional and three-dimensional perspective rotations of letters, abstract shapes, and depictions of objects (e.g. Cooper, 1976, 1991; Cooper & Shepard, 1973; Corballis, 1986).

The effect is interpreted as suggesting that subjects mentally rotate their images of the objects in an analogue fashion, until the two objects match in their orientation. The process of mental rotation is thought to be similar to the process of actual rotation of objects that are physically

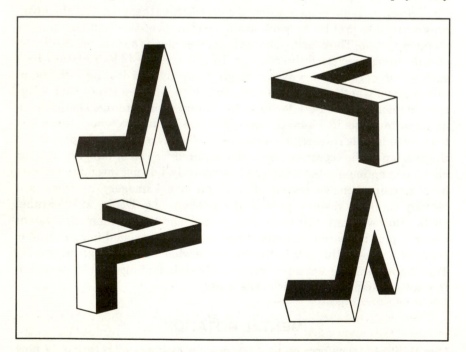

FIG. 2.1. Examples of the kind of stimuli used in the Shepard and Metzler (1971) experiments on mental rotation.

present; the greater the discrepancy in orientation, the longer it takes to rotate them into the same orientation. The fact that the relationship is linear between angle of rotation and time to rotate suggests that the images go through gradually changing intermediate states, just as they would if the subject were viewing the object.

MENTAL SCANNING

Similar findings to those reported in mental rotation experiments have been obtained in experiments where subjects are required to scan rather than rotate a mental image. For example, Kosslyn, Ball, and Reiser (1978) presented subjects with a map of a fictitious island which they were to memorise in the form of a mental image. On the island were a number of landmarks such as a hut, a marsh, a well, and so on. Once the picture of the map had been removed, subjects had to imagine a particular location on the map, and mentally scan from that location to a second named location. The subjects had to press a button when they had "arrived" at the second location, and the time taken for the mental scanning was recorded. Kosslyn and his colleagues found that scanning times were closely associated with the physical distance between the two locations on the map. Similar results have been obtained when subjects are given verbal descriptions of the maps, and are required to generate their image from the description (e.g. Denis & Cocude, 1989). The fact that similar results are obtained from a real map and from a verbal description has been interpreted to suggest that there is an equivalence between images constructed from descriptions and those based on memories for pictorial stimuli. However, in both kinds of experiments, the process of mental scanning was considered to be entirely analogous to the process of visually scanning a real scene.

This last interpretation was not without its critics, the most prolific of whom, Pylyshyn (1984), noted that subjects also have tacit knowledge about visual scanning rates and that this tacit knowledge may cause them to emulate real visual scanning. This process of emulation would allow subjects to fulfil their own expectancies about the task as well as those of the experimenters. For example Mitchell and Richman (1980) partly replicated the Kosslyn et al. map imaging task, but instead of asking subjects to perform mental scanning, they were asked to *estimate* the scanning times. Subjects' estimates matched very closely the imaged scanning times reported by Kosslyn.

There are a number of other studies which are less prone to the possible effects of tacit knowledge. Finke and Pinker (1982) presented subjects with four dots on a screen. The dots were then removed, and subjects were asked to image the locations of the dots. An arrow then appeared in an unexpected orientation and location, and subjects were asked to decide whether the arrow was pointing to the location of one of the previously presented dots. Response times increased linearly with increasing distance between the arrow and the dot location. This seems to suggest that subjects were using some form of mental scanning operation to perform the task, even although they were not specifically instructed to do so.

Podgorny and Shepard (1978) reported a similar finding in an experiment where they displayed a letter which then disappeared, to be replaced by a set of dots. Subjects were to decide whether the dots fell on or off the locations originally covered by the letter. This kind of paradigm has been adapted to tackle the possible role of tacit knowledge of perception in these tasks. Kosslyn, Cave, Provost, and von Gierke (1988) noted for example that results from imagery experiments do not necessarily always mimic results from the same task based on visual perception. Kosslyn et al. (1988) carried out an experiment of this kind where a letter was presented in lower case. The screen was then blank for 500ms followed by the display of two x-marks. Subjects were asked to imagine whether the x-marks would appear on an upper case version of the previously presented lower case letter. As with the studies by Podgorny and Shepard and by Finke and Pinker, the further away the two x-marks were from each other, the longer people took to make their decision. However when the subjects were asked to perform the same task with the upper case letter physically present, the relative position of the x-marks made no difference to decision times. This result undermines the suggestion that subjects merely emulate visual perception when they are performing mental scanning tasks.

This argument for mental scanning has been extended to suggest that images also take time to construct and that different parts of the image are constructed in sequential order. In the study described earlier Kosslyn et al. (1988) found that decision times were longer when the letters that subjects had to generate were more complex. Moreover different parts of the letter were mentally generated after different time delays. This was assessed by first noting the sequential order in which different parts of letters are normally drawn by subjects. In their subsequent experiment, when the x-marks appeared on segments of the letters that are normally drawn first, response times were faster than when the x-marks appeared on segments of the letters that are normally drawn last. That is, subjects generate images of the different segments of letters in the same sequential order as they would produce those letters when physically drawing them.

MENTAL COMPARISONS

A third topic that fuelled the debate as to the functional properties of mental images stemmed from studies of mental comparative judgements. Here, subjects are given the names of objects and asked to compare the objects according to their size, colour, weight, and so on (e.g. Whale–Goat, —which is bigger?). Subjects may be given the names of animals or objects that they have encountered outside the laboratory (e.g. Paivio, 1975). Alternatively subjects may be required in the laboratory to learn the relative sizes (or positions on some dimension) of items in a set of stimuli and are then given the names of pairs of stimuli for comparison (e.g. Moyer & Bayer, 1976; Potts, 1972, 1974). The general finding in these experiments is that the closer together a pair of items are on the dimension in question (e.g. physical size), the longer subjects take to make up their minds as to which of the pair is the larger, heavier, and so on. This has been referred to as the *symbolic distance effect* (Moyer & Bayer, 1976), and it mimics a similar finding for comparisons among pairs of items that are physically present (e.g. Curtis, Paulos, & Rule, 1973; Woodworth & Schlosberg, 1954).

The debate in this literature focused on the extent to which subjects image the objects or animals concerned rather than basing their comparative judgements on semantic knowledge of the physical characteristics. Thus subjects might image the objects in their correct relative sizes and make a judgement just as they would if the objects were physically present. The symbolic distance effect then arises because objects that are similar in size in the real world are also similar in size in the image, thus taxing the subject's ability to make an image-based psychophysical judgement (Moyer, 1973; Moyer & Bayer, 1976; Paivio, 1975). Other studies showed symbolic distance effects in comparisons of the ferocity or friendliness of animals (Kerst & Howard, 1977; Potts, 1974), and judgements of the angle between the hands of a clock for times presented as digits (Paivio, 1978). The conclusion that imagery was heavily involved in these judgements was supported by the finding that when subjects are shown pictures of the objects rather than their names, decision times are a great deal faster. This picture superiority effect was interpreted by suggesting that pictures have easier access to the imagery system than do words, thus allowing for faster processing times. This in turn seemed to support the functional role for imagery in these tasks.

There are a couple of problems with this interpretation. One issue concerns the role of semantic knowledge, the other concerns the picture superiority effect. Dealing first with semantic knowledge, subjects have access to information about size and other characteristics of objects. Thus we know that elephants are large things and mice are small things. Therefore when asked which is the larger, an elephant or a mouse, we can make this judgement purely on the basis of their smallness or largeness without recourse to visual imagery. Moreover, in order to generate an image of the items at the appropriate relative size we must have access to the relevant size information, and this raises the question of why images are needed at all. This kind of argument was raised by Banks and Flora (1977;

see also Banks, 1977; Banks, Fujii, & Kayra-Stuart, 1976). One other, related phenomenon that was reported in mental comparison studies is the *semantic congruity effect* (Banks, 1977). This refers to the finding that when subjects are to decide which of two items is the smaller, responses are faster when both objects could be considered small in some absolute sense. That is subjects would be faster deciding as to the smaller of the pair Mouse–Ant, than they would be deciding as to which was the larger of the same pair. A complementary phenomenon is associated with decisions as to which is the larger of two large objects. The semantic congruity effect was presented as evidence undermining an imagery explanation, because it was argued that semantic congruity would be more likely to have an effect on linguistic processing (Clark, 1969) rather than imaginal processing. Further, a number of studies demonstrated that the symbolic distance effect was observed even when subjects were asked to make comparative judgements on more abstract dimensions such as the cost of cars, the ferocity of animals, the military power of countries (Kerst & Howard, 1977), units of time, units of temperature, measures of quality (Holyoak & Walker, 1976), and relative friendliness (Potts, 1974). In comparisons on these dimensions, imagery would ostensibly be rather less useful.

One counter to the argument put forward by Banks and his colleagues is that some characteristics of objects may be encoded only implicitly and that one function of imagery is to make these characteristics explicit. In other words, it is possible that the *relative* size of whales and elephants is not encoded explicitly in semantic knowledge because subjects have never explicitly compared these animals prior to the experiment. They know about the size of an elephant possibly in relation to the size of themselves, and similarly they have some explicit information about the size of whales. Only when the two animals are imaged together is it possible to "discover" which of the two is the larger.

It is possible to handle the effects based on abstract dimensions in at least two ways. One is to suggest that subjects generate images that contain attributes relevant to the dimension in question. Thus subjects can make judgements of cost by, for example, imaging a very plush-looking Rolls Royce which is large with gold trimmings versus a Volkswagen Beetle which is small and notably devoid of trimmings. Similarly animals can be imaged at various levels of ferocity, and one can imagine armies and weaponry piled high in maps of the countries concerned, or pairs of temperatures on a thermometer.

An alternative view is that the symbolic distance effect may arise from the use of imagery but not uniquely so. Thus psychophysical functions are obtained with comparisons on any dimension among stimuli that are physically present, whether it involves visual, auditory, tactile, or olfactory judgements; so too *mental* comparisons may result in psychophysical functions reflected in the symbolic distance effect. Therefore these mental comparisons may involve imagery or they may not, and the presence of a symbolic distance effect may be necessary evidence but is not sufficient evidence for an involvement of imagery.

The interpretation of the picture superiority effect is also more complex than might have been thought at first. For example, pictures would not only make it easier to generate images, but they also make size information explicit and much less ambiguous than do object referents such as names. For example whales vary in size in the real world and so do elephants, and so asking subjects to determine which is the larger of the two presents a dilemma. That is, the question could be rephrased to ask whether the modal size for whales is greater than the modal size for elephants. As far as I know there are no experiments that have addressed the issue of size distribution among the objects in the real world. For example, in his 1975 paper Paivio asked a group of subjects to rate the sizes of 176 real-world objects and animals. He reported both the means and the standard deviations of the size ratings, but in his experiments he concentrated on the mean ratings. An interesting study would be to examine whether those objects with a small amount of variability in the ratings produced shorter response times than did items for which subjects gave less consistent size ratings. That is, "closeness" in physical size may be determined by the extent to which the size distributions overlap for the objects in the real world. Thus the size distributions for real ants and real mice do not overlap, whereas the size distributions for real domestic cats and real domestic dogs do overlap, although most dogs are larger than most cats that we are likely to encounter.

IMAGES, PROPOSITIONS, AND STRATEGIES

The whole area of mental comparisons was highly popular in the 1970s and early 1980s, but there is very little more recent work on the topic (e.g. Cech, 1989; Fuchs, Goschke, & Gude, 1988; Henderson & Well, 1985; Shoben, Cech, Schwanenflugel, & Sailor, 1989) despite the tractability of the procedure. This is not so much because all of the questions have been answered, far from it, but seems more to do with a combination of changing scientific fashions in the face of novel methodologies, and arguments that seemed to suggest the debate in this area was asking the wrong questions. Related recent work has concentrated more on the general issue of images as mental representations which contain the attributes of objects (e.g. Cave & Kosslyn, 1989) or on the effects of explicit size information on the picture superiority effect (Mohr & Engelkamp, 1991; Richardson, 1987). The mental comparison literature was very much a focus for the debate as to whether mental represen.ations involved some analcgue of the real world in the form of mental imagery, or whether information was represented in some form of propositional coding.

One argument that had a significant impact on this debate was voiced by Anderson (1978) who claimed that it was in principle impossible to distinguish between the two theories of mental representation purely on the basis of empirical data. His case was based on the argument that, given a set of inputs presented to two quite different systems, it was possible for both systems to produce identical outputs thus making it impossible to discern the internal workings of the two systems on the basis of their output alone. In other words a propositionally based system and an analogue based system could result in the same pattern of data output implying that the debate in the literature was really a rather futile endeavour.

However Anderson's remarks tended to finesse the problem rather than attempting to solve it. Instead of thinking about it as an impossible question to answer, it may be better to think of it as the wrong question. The division of opinion also starts with the assumption that use of particular cognitive functions are obligatory for all subjects confronted with an apparently well-designed laboratory task. A more positive approach to resolving the dispute might be to consider how a subject would approach a mental comparison task. Human beings have available semantic knowledge of the world, and many people do report using images to manipulate that knowledge. They also have other techniques available for manipulating that knowledge, such as verbal linguistic skills. When given a task to perform, a rational subject would adopt whatever technique they feel is appropriate for the task in hand from among those techniques that they have available. Thus when asked to compare the size of an elephant and of a mouse, we can use our semantic knowledge of bigness and smallness to respond without any requirement to process very much more about the properties of elephants and mice. We may even have the relative size information available from our semantic knowledge base, as elephants and mice often occur together in children's stories and in films. When the relevant size information is not available to us directly we can then attempt to process what we know about the items concerned and in the case of a physical comparison such as size, visual imagery is a rational strategy to adopt. Thus individual subjects may or may not adopt an imagery strategy depending on the demands of the task for them.

In reading the literature on this topic one highly pertinent observation is that researchers rarely report the patterns of data for individual subjects. Almost invariably conclusions are drawn on statistical grounds from aggregate data from groups of individuals. In other words, the results that are reported summarise what is true for most of the people most of the time in a particular experiment. This in turn lends support to the view that there is a functional cognitive architecture that is common to most if not all normal subjects, and which is necessary to support the cognitive processing involved in performing the task in hand. What is often missed is that in many experiments there are some subjects who do not consistently show the pattern observed for the group as a whole. Thus some subjects may fail to show a pattern that is statistically robust and reliable in the group means. Conversely, some subjects may show a pattern that is not shown by the majority, and researchers vary widely in the extent to which this information is reported.

For example one issue that crops up in some studies is that a small number of subjects produce data patterns that are sufficiently different from those of the remainder of the group to undermine the statistical significance of the group result. The relevant group effect often achieves significance when the data for these particular subjects are omitted. A common, and statistically perfectly legitimate, strategy is to omit such data from the analyses.

Thus even in those papers where they are reported, variation in performance among individual subjects or within one individual from one trial to the next is typically classified as contributing to error variance. As long as the error variance is not large these individual quirks in performance tend to be ignored. This is unfortunate because it neglects important questions as to the generality of the effects. Furthermore it is important to consider the reasons for the appearance of aberrant data from a few subjects. For example, some subjects may be very slow or error-prone, but still perform the task in the same way as the rest of the group. Alternatively, the "aberrant" subjects may be performing the task in a fashion that is qualitatively different from that of the majority, for example by using an alternative strategy. In the former case, an individual subject may not show the group effect because their performance is at floor. In the latter case, the subject's performance may reflect the operation of rather different aspects of their functional cognitive architecture.

It is also possible that there are more than just one or two errant subjects. In principle a substantial minority of subjects may fail to "conform" and yet a significant main effect may appear in the group statistics. It is rarely clear from group studies what proportion of normal subjects fit with the group pattern, and to what extent individual subjects reliably show the group effects on different occasions. Moreover the tendency to use college students in experiments may result in a very conservative estimate of the number of such "aberrant" subjects in the general population. For example, visual imagery mnemonics are widely reported to improve memory performance (see e.g. McDaniel & Pressley, 1987; Paivio, 1971). However, Wagner (1978) has argued that use of mnemonics is dependent on culture, while Richardson (1987) has shown that mnemonics only benefit memory performance in people from the higher socio-economic classes.

One legitimate reaction to these questions is that they may be of some minor interest but that they are not crucial to the development of general theories of cognition. In particular they need not undermine the assumption of a common cognitive architecture. For example, many studies may not report individual variability among their subject samples because the same data pattern was observed in all of the subjects tested. When variability does occur, simple losses of concentration in some subjects may account for the majority of error variance. However other reasons for variability may stem from the use of strategies by individual subjects. They may reliably attempt to perform the task in an idiosyncratic way, or fail to follow experimental instructions. Under some circumstances such individuals may not pose a serious problem for interpreting the experimental data as long as they comprise only a small minority of subjects. However it is also true that reliable idiosyncrasies may be highly informative.

The importance of strategy choice by subjects was pointed out in a paper by Siegler (1987) in studies of mental arithmetic. Also in some studies by my colleague Sergio Della Sala and myself, we have shown that the widely reported and statistically robust phenomena of phonological similarity and word length in short-term verbal memory tasks are not shown by a substantial minority of the general population (Della Sala, Logie, Marchetti, & Wynn, 1991; Logie, Della Sala, Laiacona, Chalmers, & Wynn, submitted). Moreover people vary as to whether they show these effects from one occasion to the next. Thus people do not all perform mental arithmetic tasks or short-term verbal memory tasks in the same way, nor do all people when confronted by the same task necessarily rely on the same aspects of their cognitive architecture.

To return to the issue of mental representation, it would be interesting to ask of studies reporting support for the importance of imaginal processes, how many subjects in the group produced the data pattern reported for the group as a whole. The same question could be asked of studies that claimed to support a propositionally based processing system. Thus subjects may use either a propositionally based cognitive process drawing on semantic and linguistic knowledge or they may use an imagery-based cognitive process depending on the task set before them. This does not undermine the possibility that these processes form part of the functional cognitive architecture of all subjects. It merely states that people are more flexible than cognitive psychologists have given them credit for as to which parts of that functional cognitive architecture they employ for a given task. The imagery/propositional debate then is transformed into a discussion about which of the available strategies most subjects favour for the tasks set in a particular experiment.

Whether or not this provides a definitive resolution for the debate it does seem that a more fruitful way forward might be to view the scientific endeavour of cognitive psychology as attempting to discern the characteristics of the various forms of cognitive function that human beings have available to them. This seems closer to the characteristics of human cognition than to assume that all subjects perform the same tasks in the same way. Thus averaging data from groups of individuals is still perfectly legitimate provided we are sure that in doing so the aggregate pattern is not an artefact of the averaging process. Specifically, how many subjects show the majority pattern and how many do not? Nor should we fall into the trap of mounting a major debate about the nature of human cognition on the basis of differential patterns of data from different experiments that may well reflect differential strategy choice by subjects. The issue of strategy choice in visual imagery tasks crops up in the next section on discoveries from imagery.

DISCOVERIES FROM IMAGES

A obvious question to ask is what the imagery system might be used for outside of cleverly designed laboratory experiments. Mental scanning, mental comparisons, and mental rotation clearly are cognitive abilities that could be useful if applied to tasks in everyday life. Imagining a route to follow through a town can aid navigation (e.g. Robin & Denis, 1991). So too, being able to image an object in its correct size may allow us to search for that object more successfully. Trying to find a building in a town can be a lot easier if we can generate in advance an image of the building from a verbal description of its size relative to neighbouring buildings. Likewise trying to find a four-centimetre nail among a pile of nails of varying sizes is much easier if we can create an image of the nail in its correct size before starting the search (e.g. Cave & Kosslyn, 1989; Larsen & Bundesen, 1978). Also, manipulating an image (e.g. by rotation) of an object may allow us to discover properties of the object that were not obvious from its initial depiction or orientation (Brandimonte, Hitch, & Bishop, 1992a,b; Finke, Pinker, & Farah, 1989; Finke & Slayton, 1988).

Some of the best known studies on "discovery" from images were conducted by Finke and Slayton (1988). In their experiments subjects were asked to construct a mental image of letters and combine the letters in ways that might lead to a novel configuration and interpretation. For example, subjects might be asked to imagine a capital letter J, and then to imagine a capital letter D alongside. They then had to rotate the D anticlockwise by 90 degrees and place it on top of the J, so that the straight edge of the D and the top bar of the J coincided. Finally subjects were to report a verbal label for the resulting image, which in this case resembles a two-dimensional picture of an umbrella.

A complementary set of experiments was conducted by Brandimonte, Hitch, and Bishop (1992a,b) who presented subjects with pictures of objects, along with a picture of one segment of the object. In one experiment, the subject's task was to image the object, and then to subtract the pictured segment from their image. An example of the kind of stimuli used is shown in Fig. 2.2 where a wrapped sweet (candy) is shown along with a picture of one end of the sweet. If the pictured part of the sweet is subtracted, the resulting image would resemble a picture of a fish as shown in the lower part of the figure. That is, subjects can "discover" an image of a fish by reconstruing their image of a "part of a sweet".

The fact that subjects can perform these kinds of tasks suggests that novel discoveries can indeed be made from images. The results also fit with the earlier studies on mental rotation which in a sense involve a "discovery" that the pictured object matches a target figure when mentally rotated. Similarly, in the mental comparison studies subjects are making mental discoveries as to the relative size of the objects portrayed in the image.

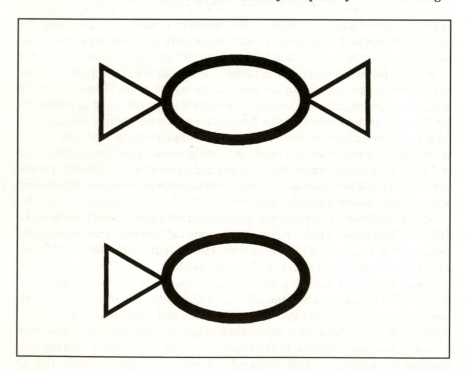

FIG. 2.2. An example of the kind of stimuli for the mental addition and mental subtraction experiments by Brandimonte et al. (1992a;b).

What is interesting about this area however is that there do appear to be limits on when people can make discoveries. For a number of the Finke and Slayton stimuli, subjects are unable to come up with an appropriate descriptive label for the resulting image. Similarly, some of the Brandimonte et al. stimuli cause difficulties for some subjects. One possible response to this would be that the resulting images are inherently difficult to name, or that the stimuli are too complex to retain and manipulate in the form of visual images.

Some insight into this comes from some further studies by Brandimonte et al. (1992a;b) where they showed that when subjects are asked to repeat an irrelevant word (articulatory suppression) during the mental subtraction task, then performance improves somewhat, but only for pictures of objects that are easy to name. They interpret these findings by suggesting that subjects spontaneously name the pictures with which they are presented, whenever this is possible, but that naming gets in the way of generating an image and performing the task in the most optimal way —that is, by relying primarily on imagery rather than verbal codes. When subjects are suppressing articulation they are less likely to rely on these verbal codes and more likely to rely on visual imagery, resulting in better performance. For pictures that are difficult to name, subjects do not attempt to use verbal codes in any case, and articulatory suppression has no effect.

This is an attractive result in many ways in that it highlights some of the comments I made earlier about subjects having available a number of strategies, and that they select the strategy that seems most appropriate for the task in hand. Apparently a verbally based strategy is not optimal for the Brandimonte et al. task, and yet many of her subjects chose spontaneously to use such a strategy. It also points to at least one of the constraints on discovery from images. That is, given the opportunity to use verbal codes subjects may do so, even if a more optimal strategy (that would allow discoveries) is available to them.

There are however circumstances under which subjects find it extremely difficult if not impossible to reconstrue images or to make discoveries from images. This crops up in studies of ambiguous figures. The seminal paper on this topic was published by Chambers and Reisberg (1985) who showed subjects pictures of ambiguous figures such as the duck–rabbit shown in Fig. 2.3. When subjects are given an unlimited amount of time to look at this figure they report "reversals" such that initially they may see the figure as depicting a rabbit, and a little while later will see it as a depicting a duck. These two perceptual interpretations continue to alternate while the figure is in view.

Results are rather different for subjects who are shown the figure for the first time for a period of just five seconds. When subjects were then

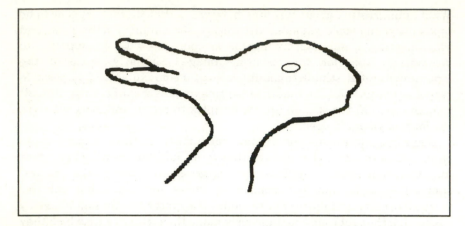

FIG. 2.3. Example of the form of the ambiguous duck–rabbit figure.

asked about their interpretation of the figure, some reported that the figure depicted a rabbit and some reported imaging a duck. However, even after prompting, none of the subjects reported the reversals that are almost invariably reported when the stimulus is physically present. Those initially reporting a duck in their image continued to report a duck, and conversely for those initially reporting a rabbit. They were nevertheless able to report the alternate interpretation when, a few moments later, they were asked to draw their image on paper and they looked at their drawing.

Here, then, was a case when subjects were clearly unable to make a discovery or to reconstrue their image, and the results are remarkably clear. Reisberg and his colleagues have shown similar phenomena when subjects are shown apparently abstract shapes, which they then have to mentally rotate. Unknown to the subjects some of the stimuli fit with familiar outlines when rotated appropriately such as the shape of Africa or of the state of Texas (Reisberg & Chambers, 1991). Subjects fail to recognise the shape as Africa or Texas from their rotated image but can do so from their own drawings of their image.

Reisberg argues (see e.g. Reisberg, in press) that images do more than just depict; they have in addition an associated frame of reference, and discoveries cannot occur from images when such discoveries require a change in the frame of reference for the image. The abstract shapes are exactly that. They are not only abstract, but also they have an assignment of what is figure and what is background, and have certain geometric properties such as a "top" and a "right" and "left" side. Moreover, they have an organisation that dictates which features are most salient for the particular construal in hand. Thus the duck interpretation of Fig. 2.3 would have as salient features the beak and the eye. The small indentation on the back of the head would be considered irrelevant. On the other hand, the rabbit would require a reconstrual of the beak as a "pair of ears", and have the indentation as a salient feature that constitutes its mouth. In the case of the abstract shapes, discovery of the outline maps requires a shift in the reference frame and in particular, following rotation of the image, subjects have to reassign which side of the figure constitutes the "top", the "bottom", and the "right" and "left" sides. Only when subjects are explicitly told to "reassign which side is the top" in their image do a number report discovery of the map of Texas or of Africa. That is, reconstrual requires a change in the reference frame and this requirement poses considerable difficulty for most subjects.

Other researchers have shown similar failures by subjects to report spontaneous reversals in images of ambiguous figures (e.g. Brandimonte & Gerbino, 1993; Kaufmann & Helstrup, 1993), although in their case a small number of subjects do discover the alternative image.

One possible interpretation of these findings is that subjects are using verbal labels for the pictures, and this undermines depiction of the relevant features in the image. For example, when subjects are shown the duck–rabbit figure they may verbally encode the picture as being that of a duck, and not create an image at all. When later asked to create an image, they generate this from the information in their long-term memory about the visual features of ducks, perhaps incorporating in their image those features that they can remember from the original stimulus. Some evidence for this view was reported by Brandimonte and Gerbino (1993) who presented subjects with the duck–rabbit figure while they were instructed to suppress articulation by repeating "la la la". Under these conditions an appreciable number of subjects did report spontaneous reversals; a result which is analogous to that obtained by Brandimonte et al. (1992a;b) with the mental subtraction task. In response Reisberg (in press) has noted that articulatory suppression only assists reconstrual of the image when subjects have to suppress articulation during encoding of the duck–rabbit stimulus, and when the stimulus is in view for only two seconds. If the stimulus is in view for longer or if suppression occurs only during the subsequent imaging phase then there is no benefit derived from articulatory suppression.

The logic of the Brandimonte and Gerbino studies is that articulatory suppression not only suppresses subvocal articulation, but also suppresses the generation of a name for the object depicted in the visual stimulus. The original use of articulatory suppression was of course as a technique for disrupting, if not preventing, subvocal rehearsal of a verbal sequence and the relevant data on this are clear (Levy, 1971; Murray, 1968). That is, most of the studies that have used articulatory suppression have focused on its relationship with subvocal rehearsal, with phonological coding, and with articulation. These studies have not addressed the task of object naming, and the argument that articulatory suppression prevents naming is not persuasive. This is easy to demonstrate if you repeat an irrelevant word out loud and attempt mentally to name objects around you. The phenomenal experience provides a compelling argument that articulatory suppression clearly does not stop the mental generation of the names for objects. In an analogous fashion, it is already well established that articulatory suppression does not block access to the phonology of printed words (e.g. Baddeley & Lewis, 1981; Besner, 1987; for a review see Baddeley & Logie, 1992). Articulatory suppression may however discourage the use of object names when attempting to *retain* information about a visually presented stimulus. That is, subvocal rehearsal may be involved when we have to retain verbal codes over a short period of time, although it may not be involved in initial retrieval of the verbal label from long-term memory. Thus, as argued earlier in this chapter, subjects may be strategic in their approach to performing the task, and attempting the task under articulatory suppression may encourage them to seek and adopt a strategy that is not based on naming.

There is a lot we do not know about the range of influence of articulatory suppression. For example in the imaging tasks described earlier the effect may not be specifically on naming, but may act as a form of general distraction which somehow undermines the establishment of a perceptual reference frame. The argument here would go along the following lines. Articulatory suppression occupies the system responsible for the production of articulate speech, and this same system is used in the retention of sequences of verbal items. However articulatory suppression also requires the use of a more general-purpose cognitive resource, such as the central executive of working memory, to initiate its activity and to ensure that it keeps going. The extent of the executive demand may vary from one person to another, and therefore some subjects may attend to the articulatory productions more than others. The fact that attentional resource is directed towards articulatory suppression rather than the visually displayed stimulus may affect the normal course of processing of visual stimuli, particularly if the stimuli are ambiguous and their interpretation is not automatic. In order to perceive such an object, and thereby to establish its perceptual reference frame, we also require attentional resource, some of which is allocated to the suppression task. As a result the reference frame is not fully established and the image of the stimulus retains its ambiguity. Because there is an element of ambiguity in the image, this allows the image to be reinterpreted once suppression has ceased, and indeed the advantage is obtained when articulatory suppression is required only during initial presentation. This would then provide an account of the increase in the number of subjects who report reconstruals.

In the same vein it is notable that only a small majority of Brandimonte and Gerbino's subjects benefited from articulatory suppression in this way —a substantial minority did not. This data pattern is consistent with the interpretation given earlier, of the strategic allocation of attention by some subjects. The trouble with this interpretation of course is that it is somewhat ad hoc; however it is not untestable. It predicts for example that other forms of distracting task also will benefit imagery-based reconstrual of the duck–rabbit figure. Brandimonte and Gerbino made an initial attempt to test this hypothesis by using concurrent hand tapping instead of articulatory suppression. They obtained no improvement in reconstruals of the duck–rabbit figure and concluded that the effects of articulatory suppression were specific rather than general. Unfortunately this does not settle the issue, as the failure to find a significant improvement in performance with concurrent tapping can be interpreted in terms of the differential difficulty of the concurrent tasks. Moreover, in previous studies, concurrent tapping has been shown to disrupt imagery tasks (e.g. Farmer, Berman, & Fletcher, 1986; Quinn & Ralston, 1986). That is, the effect of concurrent tapping may be twofold; one is that it acts as a general distraction, but unlike articulatory suppression it also has a specific interference effect on the ability of subjects to maintain the detailed visual information necessary for reconstrual. Thus, with concurrent tapping, the subjects may not have a well-formed perceptual frame of reference which would increase the likelihood of reconstrual, but they may also not be able to retain, say, the detail of the bump on the back of the duck's head which would allow them to reinterpret the image as a rabbit.

This discussion is necessarily speculative but the debate is more to do with the role of imagery in creativity and discovery than specifically about visuo-spatial working memory. Nevertheless, the issues at stake are very much part of the contemporary imagery literature, and have a bearing on some of the arguments in this book. For these reasons I have introduced here the salient points and the flavour of the debate. A full discussion of this debate is given in Cornoldi, Logie, Brandimonte, Kaufmann, and Reisberg (in press).

To return then to the main topic of this book, how does all of this work on mental imagery link up with the range of work on visuo-spatial working memory? Certainly one of the original claims about the visuo-spatial scratch pad was that it provided a medium for visual imagery as well as for temporary visual memory (Baddeley, 1986; Baddeley, Grant, Wight, & Thomson, 1975; Baddeley & Lieberman, 1980; Logie, 1986). Note however that in all the imagery tasks described here, and in many more besides, the mental representations incorporate semantics. Images are images of something. They are not raw visual impressions, even when they are images of recently presented pictures or objects. Therefore if it is the case that the visuo-spatial scratch pad is closely involved in imagery tasks, its contents incorporate information that is not available from the pure visual features of the presented object. Even in the case of the duck–rabbit, irrespective of which side of the debate you are on, the image at any one moment has some associated meaning, even if this meaning is generic, for example "depicts a living creature". Therefore the generation of an image in visuo-spatial working memory cannot be accomplished from visual input alone, but requires access to long-term memory representations that are concerned with the properties of the perceived visual input. If Reisberg is right that each image has an associated perceptual reference frame, the generation of this reference frame also must involve access to long-term memory representations. This adds fuel to the case against a gateway property for working memory raised in Chapter 1. A further key issue is whether the system involved in temporary visual storage and that involved in visual imagery tasks (and imagery reconstrual) are one and the same. This remains a largely untested assumption that I shall start to explore in Chapter 3.

CHAPTER THREE

The Visual and The Spatial

In Chapter 1, I presented some of the evidence supporting the existence of a specialised short-term memory system, and briefly discussed the kinds of tasks that might involve a temporary *visuo-spatial* memory system. However, the case for such a specialised memory system is far from convincing on the basis of these data alone. Indeed in the 1993 Bartlett Lecture at the University of Toronto, Endel Tulving stated that he knew of no convincing evidence for a specialised visuo-spatial short-term memory system. This presents something of a challenge to researchers in the area, and as such may be a very effective way of provoking further activity on the topic.

The coverage of the key issues and studies in the imagery literature in Chapter 2 was intended to set the scene for asking whether data from imagery studies might help build a case for a specialised visuo-spatial temporary memory system. This makes intuitive sense, as the generation and retention of visual images ought to involve a visual short-term memory system. There is indeed a literature which explores this link. It comprises a range of studies that have developed in the context of working memory, and which have attempted to illuminate the *cognitive functions* that might host the phenomenal experience of images and imagery manipulation. They have also focused on the retention of images and of visually presented material. In contrast, the literature alluded to in Chapter 2 focused on the phenomena of imagery and imagery manipulation. In those latter studies the emphasis was on *imagery* systems rather than more general visuo-spatial memory and processing systems which may, among other things, play a central role in imagery tasks.

In this chapter then, I shall describe some of the studies that have attempted to explore the link between visual imagery and visuo-spatial working memory.

READING, LISTENING, AND VISUALISATION

A series of studies carried out by Brooks in the late 1960s provided a very useful set of techniques for studying visualisation, which have been widely adopted in studying visual working memory. In one set of studies, Brooks (1968) asked subjects to visualise a block capital letter, and to imagine each of the corners going in a clockwise direction around the letter shape. If the corner was on the outside of the figure the subject had to respond "Yes". If the corner was on the inside of the figure the subject had to respond "No". The response was indicated in one of two ways: either the subjects responded vocally, or they responded by pointing to the words "yes" or "no" which they saw printed at random positions on a sheet of paper. For the example shown in Fig. 3.1, starting from the top left-hand corner, the correct series of responses would be "Yes, Yes, No, No, Yes, Yes, Yes, Yes, No, No, Yes, Yes".

What Brooks found was that subjects performed more poorly when pointing to a printed word, than when they had to speak their response. This result was in contrast to that for a complementary task where the

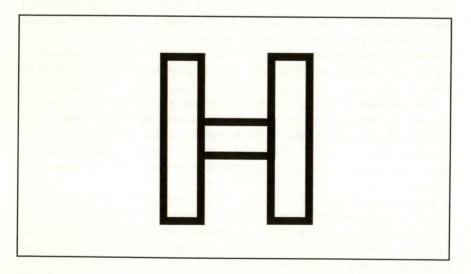

FIG. 3.1. Example of the form of the stimulus used in the Brooks (1968) experiments.

response methods were the same as before, but where subjects had to classify the words of a phrase as to whether or not they were nouns. Thus for the phrase "A bird in the hand is not in the bush", a correct series of responses would be "No, Yes, No, No, Yes, No, No, No, No, Yes". With this task, Brooks found that subjects had more difficulty responding vocally than they did when pointing, the reverse of the result for the letter task.

Brooks interpreted these results by suggesting that visualising a block capital letter appeared to use cognitive resources that were also required for reading and pointing to printed words, and that the requirement to do both led to a conflict, and to poorer performance. Where subjects were visualising but were responding vocally presumably there was less of an overlap in the cognitive resources required, and better performance resulted. The same argument would hold for the word classification task, namely that deciding which of a series of words were nouns used cognitive resources that were also required for vocalising a response, leading to poorer performance than when subjects responded by pointing.

Brooks (1967) reported a further set of studies where in one condition, subjects were asked to imagine placing consecutive numbers in consecutive squares of a visualised matrix. A example is shown in Fig. 3.2. Subjects were always to start in the second row and second column of a four by four square matrix, and the subject either read and listened, or only listened to the instructions as to which square came next in the sequence. Once the presented sequence was complete subjects responded with verbatim vocal recall of the series of sentences.

A complementary condition was devised where subjects again had to retain a sequence of sentences, except that the words "up, down, left, and right" were replaced by the words "good, bad, slow, and quick". This resulted in a set of nonsense sentences which were to be retained without the use of any form of visual image, perhaps by subvocal rehearsal. As before subjects either listened to and read, or just listened to the sentences.

The pattern of results was very similar to that for the previous experiment. When subjects were asked to remember the positions of numbers in an imagined matrix their performance was poorer if they had to read and listen to the sentences describing those positions than if they had only to listen to the sentences. This was not true for the set of nonsense sentences.

One possible explanation for these results is that the visual imaging tasks and/or the visual perceptual processing were simply more difficult than were the verbal storage and auditory processing tasks. Combining two difficult tasks is likely to lead to poorer performance than for two easier tasks. This explanation falls down if we consider the set of results from the Brooks (1968) experiment, where in one condition the visualised letter task was disrupted, whereas in the complementary condition the verbal

	1	**2**	
	4	**3**	**8**
	5	**6**	**7**

In the first square put a 1
In the next square to the right put a 2
In the next square down put a 3
In the next square to the left put a 4
In the next square down put a 5
In the next square to the right put a 6
In the next square to the right put a 7
In the next square up put an 8

FIG. 3.2. Example trial for the Brooks (1967) matrix experiment.

classification task was disrupted. This "cross-over interaction" is fairly compelling evidence against a task difficulty hypothesis and provides support for a memory and processing system that functions somewhat independently of the system responsible for retaining verbal material. In addition the differential disruption of a visualisation task by a concurrent visual-perceptual task is consistent with the view that there is a specialised cognitive function that deals both with processing visual input and with generating and retaining images.

Therefore if visuo-spatial working memory acts primarily as an input buffer for visually presented material, it appears that this input buffer may also be involved in the construction of visual imagery representations. Conversely, if visual working memory is thought of primarily as a medium for constructing and manipulating images, it appears that this imagery manipulation system also deals with visual perceptual input. If we accept this argument then we have good reason to believe that there is a strong overlap between visuo-spatial imagery and visuo-spatial working memory.

Baddeley, Grant, Wight, and Thomson (1975) followed up the Brooks (1967) study by exploring the effect of concurrent perceptual-motor tracking on retention of the Brooks matrix or verbal (nonsense) material. Subjects heard the sequence of sentences and at the same time were required to follow a moving target. Tracking had a significantly disruptive effect on retention of the positions of numbers in the visualised matrix but had no effect on retention of the set of nonsense sentences. In sum it appeared that there was some overlap between the cognitive resources required to retain the Brooks matrix material, and those necessary for making arm movements to follow a mobile target. In other words visuo-spatial working memory not only involves visual perceptual input and visual imagery, but is also needed for the production and/or control of movement.

REMEMBERING CONCRETE AND ABSTRACT WORDS

Another potentially fruitful approach to studying the role of imagery and visuo-spatial working memory in cognition, is to explore the widely replicated finding that immediate free recall of lists of concrete words is almost invariably better than it is for lists of abstract words (e.g. Paivio & Csapo, 1969; Warren, 1977). This is true even when we take account of other factors such as word frequency. Paivio (1971) provided an explanation for this in terms of his dual coding theory. This theory suggests that for concrete words it is possible to create visual images of the object that the word represents. Thus when presented with a concrete word such as "elephant" two memory codes are generated; one is verbal and the other is a visual image of an elephant. For abstract words such as "ideal" or "intellect" it is more difficult to create a visual image, and in this case recall of the word relies on the verbal code alone. Because the concrete word generates two codes, if one code is forgotten then the other code may still be available. This form of back-up is less readily available for abstract words. (For more recent statements of dual coding theory see Paivio, 1986.) However, a number of authors have been somewhat sceptical of this interpretation of the concreteness effect.

Baddeley and his colleagues (Baddeley, Grant, Wight, & Thomson, 1975) attempted to test the Paivio dual coding model by requiring subjects to retain concrete or abstract word pairs, such as "bullet-grey" or "idea-original", and to combine this with a perceptual-motor tracking task, in which subjects had to follow a moving target with a stylus. If visual imagery is used for concrete words as Paivio suggested, then a concurrent visuo-spatial task should undermine the advantage for concrete material in the same way that concurrent tracking disrupted retention of the Brooks matrix. Baddeley et al. showed that retention of the concrete pairs was indeed superior to that for the abstract pairs, but that there was no tendency for the tracking task to differentially impair recall of the concrete pairs. A similar result was reported by Warren (1977). Baddeley et al. suggested that the memory advantage for concrete words was more likely due to the richness of the semantic content of such words rather than their imageability.

Unfortunately these data are not conclusive because the Baddeley et al. interpretation relies on the assumption that the cognitive mechanisms responsible for images derived from concrete words are the same mechanisms that are used for the Brooks matrix task and for tracking. This assumption may not be justified. For example, the Brooks matrix task involves the construction of an image of an arbitrary pattern piece by piece as the instructions are presented. This is very different from the generation of an image of a known object in response to its name. In this latter case, subjects may call on representations of specific objects that they have seen, or use semantic knowledge as to the typical characteristics of specific objects. Arbitrary patterns have less recourse to this additional source of information. So the underlying cognitions involved in the two forms of imagery task may be very different from one another. Thus there is still an arguable case that some form of imagery contributes to the concreteness effect.

Jones (1985; 1988) has tackled the issue by suggesting that the advantage for concrete words seems to be associated with the ease with which subjects can report different uses for words (ease of predication). To illustrate the concept of ease of predication, in one of his experiments (Jones, 1988), for each of 125 words subjects were asked to write down two factual statements about the word. So for example, given the word "dog" a subject might write down:

A dog is a type of animal
A dog often lives in a kennel

Subjects were to produce these statements as quickly as possible, and the time taken to write down the two statements was recorded. In an earlier study, Jones (1985) measured subjective estimates of the ease of predication by asking subjects to rate, on a seven-point scale, how easy it would be to produce simple, factual statements about the 125 words. Both rated "predicability" and time for predication correlated highly with subjective ratings of imageability and with the effectiveness of the words as cues for recall. That is, ease of predication was at least as good a predictor of recall performance as was imageability.

This leaves something of a dilemma, in that if both measures are equally good predictors then which should we choose? One line of argument would be that the high correlation between predicability and imageability indicates that they reflect essentially the same phenomena. That is, subjects can produce predicates for words because the words are easy to image as well as vice versa. For example, we can imagine a dog and our image may well be of a dog sitting in a kennel, or chasing rabbits or fetching a stick. It would be a trivial matter to generate two factual statements derived from those images. Thus the times taken to generate predicates may reflect the times required to generate images that contain enough information from which the predicates can be derived. All of the subjects in Jones' experiments showed predication times that were in excess of 18 seconds. This would be ample time to generate an image and write down two factual descriptors of that image.

One possible advantage to predication is that it provides a direct measure of performance—the number of factual statements or predicates produced. The effects of imagery can only be observed indirectly, by manipulating the stimulus materials and task instructions and then noting the effect of these manipulations on memory performance or times to produce a keypress response. However, although the measure of predication time is more direct, it relies on recording how long a subject takes to write down factual statements, and this is a relatively crude measure. Moreover Richardson (1980, pp.87,90) has argued that words with greater ease of predication not only can result in a range of verbal predicates, but also can produce visual and spatial predicates—that is, they can readily produce visual images that are richly endowed with ancillary information. Therefore imageability rather than predication persists as the more useful concept.

Another source of evidence for the link between concreteness and imagery lies in studies of neuropsychological patients. Richardson (1979; 1984) has shown that the memory advantage enjoyed by concrete words is not present in adult patients who have suffered from closed head injury. In those earlier studies he interpreted this result to suggest that the patients have a particular difficulty in generating visual images. In a later study Richardson and Barry (1985) replicated the pattern of data obtained for closed head injury patients, but demonstrated that these same patients did show a concreteness advantage when they were encouraged to use imagery. In other words, unlike normal subjects the patients with closed head injuries did not spontaneously use imagery to remember the words but could do so when instructed. This reinforces the conclusion that the advantage for concrete words specifically relies on the generation of images in response to the words.

More recent studies have suggested that the concreteness advantage for single words plays a less important role in memory for passages of text (see e.g. Marschark & Cornoldi, 1991; Marschark, Warner, Thomson, & Huffman, 1991). Marschark and his colleagues have explored the utility of the dual coding model in cases where subjects are asked to recall prose passages rather than word lists or verbal paired associates. Early studies on this topic suggested that prose passages which contain concrete referents are remembered more effectively than passages comprising primarily abstract material (e.g. Begg & Paivio, 1969; Yuille & Paivio, 1969) However it is clear that when the coherence and comprehensibility of the prose passages is controlled then the concrete advantage is removed (Marschark, 1985; Marschark & Paivio, 1977). Marschark has argued that the relational and the distinctive information in the material for recall may be more important than whether it is concrete or abstract. By distinctiveness, Marschark refers to features of an item that make it readily discriminable from other items that are to be remembered. By relational, he refers to the extent to which items for recall can be organised and integrated in memory.

Marschark has demonstrated that the relational/distinctiveness information also appears to be more important than concreteness in free recall of paired-associates (Marschark & Hunt, 1989; Marschark & Surian, 1989). It is possible that imagery may still play a role in enhancing the distinctiveness of verbal material, but it is clear that imagery is not the only factor that can serve this function in accounting for the concreteness effect. It is likely then that visuo-spatial working memory has an equally ambivalent relationship with the concreteness effect.

In contrast to the effects on *memory* for prose, it does appear that imageability is important in *comprehension* of prose. Eddy and Glass (1981) presented subjects with sentences for verification. The sentences were either concrete and highly imageable, (e.g. "The star of David has six points"), or abstract (e.g. "There are seven days in the week). When subjects had to read the sentences, verification speed was slower for the concrete sentences. An earlier study (Glass, Eddy, & Schwanenflugel, 1980) showed that reading verification was impaired when subjects had simultaneously to retain a complex visual pattern. This observation bears a close resemblance to the findings reported by Brooks (1967; 1968), which demonstrated that subjects had difficulty reading instructions while at the same time constructing and consulting images derived from those instructions.

These contrasting results for prose memory and for prose comprehension leave us with a puzzle as to how to interpret the failure of Baddeley, Grant, Wight, and Thomson (1975) to find interference effects of tracking on the concrete–abstract difference in memory tasks. The earlier discussion weakens the suggestion that the concreteness effect in memory is more to do with elaborative semantic coding as Baddeley et al. suggested, although one argument could be that distinctiveness rather than elaboration or imagery was involved in learning concrete paired-associates. There is no reason to expect a distinctiveness advantage to be disrupted by concurrent tracking any more than semantic elaboration would be. A related possibility is that imagery is involved in comprehension of highly imageable sentences, but subjects can take or leave imagery when it comes to temporary storage of the imageable material. Baddeley et al. used a memory task rather than a comprehension task, and this could be why they did not observe evidence for the use of imagery.

One other interpretation not yet considered is that the concurrent tracking task used by Baddeley and his colleagues may not have been the best test of imagery use. The logic of dual task methodology is driven by the assumption that where no mutual interference occurs under dual task conditions, it is reasonable to infer that the two tasks do not share cognitive resources. Thus the fact that tracking does not undermine the concreteness advantage in paired-associate memory tasks could indeed mean that memory for concrete words does not rely on visual imagery. Alternatively it could indicate that memory for concrete words does rely on visual imagery, but that perceptuo-motor tracking does not. If we examine cases where concurrent tracking does interfere, it does so when combined with a spatial rather than a visual primary task. For example, the Brooks matrix task is primarily a spatial task, particularly when the verbal descriptions of the matrix are presented auditorily. Thus the lack of a disruptive effect of tracking on the concreteness advantage can be handled by the simple assumption that spatial imagery and visual imagery are distinct. This assumption is relatively neutral with respect to the visual imagery explanation of the concreteness effect.

In sum, it appears that the balance of the evidence still tilts in favour of suggesting that visual imagery is implicated in the advantage in memory for lists of concrete words, in the use of concrete words as cues for recall, and in the comprehension of concrete sentences. The fact that concreteness is not a key factor in prose memory does not undermine the conclusion that imagery is involved in these other cases. Nevertheless, the equivocal status of the link between imagery and concreteness has meant that the concrete–abstract distinction has not figured widely in studies of visual working memory. Set against this is the extensive coverage given to concreteness effects in the imagery literature (see e.g. Paivio, 1991). The concept of a visual versus spatial dissociation which I touched on briefly earlier may help resolve this issue and provide additional insights. It is a distinction that I shall return to in considerably more detail in Chapter 4.

STORING VISUAL PATTERNS

In this chapter so far, I have considered the role for imagery and visuo-spatial working memory in tasks where visuo-spatial representations are constructed from verbal material. In these tasks, subjects see or hear words, and any images that are generated rely on the semantics of the word, and not for example on the visual form of the letters in the word. Like the visual imagery literature discussed in Chapter 3, research within the working memory context has also studied the retention of the visual features of visually presented stimuli. Some of the most widely cited findings on this topic were carried out by Phillips and his colleagues (e.g. Phillips, 1983; Phillips & Christie, 1977a,b). The paradigm that they developed involved presenting subjects with a sequence of square matrix patterns, with half of the cells of the matrix filled at random. An example of the kinds of patterns used is shown in Fig. 3.3.

Phillips used a recognition procedure such that after presentation of the sequence, subjects were shown patterns that were either identical to patterns previously shown, or where some change had occurred in the pattern. Their task was to identify which patterns they had seen before. Typically in these experiments, memory for the patterns was tested in reverse serial order, so that the last pattern presented was tested first. Phillips and Christie (1977a) reported a marked visual recency effect, such that the last matrix pattern presented was recognised correctly more often than were items presented earlier in the sequence. Performance was just above chance for all of the other serial positions, including the first. Phillips (e.g., 1983) has suggested that the single-item recency effect may reflect the operation of short-term visual storage, whereas what is retained of earlier items involves long-term memory. A typical result from the Phillips and Christie (1977a;b) studies is shown in Fig. 3.4.

In another set of studies Phillips and Christie (1977b) investigated the effect of secondary tasks interpolated between presentation of the last item in the series and the recognition test. The major finding was that the

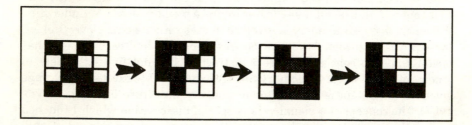

FIG. 3.3. Example of the kind of stimuli used in the Phillips and Christie (1977a;b) studies.

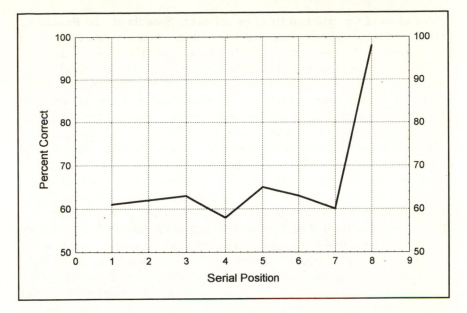

FIG. 3.4. Example of one-item recency effect from the Phillips and Christie (1977a;b) studies.

one-item visual recency effect was removed by a variety of secondary tasks, and in particular by mental arithmetic interpolated between presentation of the last item and the test of retention. Phillips and Christie argued that as mental arithmetic is unlikely to rely heavily on visualising, this result suggests that visualisation of the last matrix pattern in the series requires the use of general-purpose resources rather than a self-contained visual short-term memory system.

This conclusion has been shown subsequently to be less convincing than it might at first appear. Broadbent and Broadbent (1981) examined temporary storage of abstract, irregular patterns and wallpaper patterns. Subjects in their experiment were shown a series of such patterns followed by a probe item. On only half of the occasions was the probe item a "target" from the presented series. Target probes were selected from various positions in the series, and subjects were requested to indicate whether or not they recognised the probe item as coming from the presented series.

Under these conditions, Broadbent and Broadbent found a recency effect such that when the target was among the last three items in the series performance was much better than if target probes were selected from among those items presented earlier in the series. This "three-item" visual recency effect is in contrast to the one-item recency effect reported by Phillips and Christie.

On some of the trials in their experiment, Broadbent and Broadbent introduced a second task that was interpolated between presentation of the series and presentation of the probe. Under these conditions performance was impaired, but the disruptive effect occurred for all items in the list, and not just for the recency items. Thus the visual recency effect remained intact, again unlike the Phillips and Christie result. The Broadbents interpreted the difference in the findings of the two studies as follows. They argued that in the Phillips and Christie studies some of the non-recency matrix items could be recoded using verbal labels such as "two horizontal lines" or "looks like the letter L" (see Fig. 3.3). Only a small number of the patterns would need to be labelled in this way to generate an overall performance level that was modestly but significantly above chance (50% in Fig. 3.4) on pre-recency items. They argued further that this very modest level of performance, based on verbal labelling, would be relatively insensitive to disruption from a secondary task, whereas the higher levels of performance on the recency item would be much more vulnerable to disruption. In other words, the differential disruption of the recency item could arise because there was room for performance on that item to deteriorate, whereas performance on pre-recency items was too close to floor to allow for a further drop in performance. Therefore the Phillips and Christie result arose from an artefact of the performance levels rather than because of differential disruption of the system responsible for visual short-term storage.

The overall levels of performance in the Broadbent experiments were higher than they were for the Phillips and Christie tasks. In particular, subjects in the Broadbent task recalled more of the non-recency items, allowing scope for a deterioration in performance with the introduction of an interpolated secondary task. Thus the visual memory task in both the Broadbent and the Phillips studies may well employ general-purpose resources that are also required by the interpolated task. But these resources appear to be used equally for the pre-recency and the recency items in retention of a series of abstract patterns. That is, the advantage for the recency item cannot readily be interpreted as reflecting the use of such general-purpose resources. Therefore this visual recency effect is still consistent with the involvement of a specialised visual short-term store, and Broadbent and Broadbent concluded that their visual recency effect appeared to reflect the operation of a such a store.

In a later study Avons and Phillips (1987) examined recognition for matrix patterns either immediately after a brief display (short-term visual memory) or following visual interference (long-term visual memory). They found evidence for coding of matrices as shape descriptions and by means of semantic classification, depending on the conditions of the experiment. This lends support to the Broadbent and Broadbent suggestion that subjects in the earlier Phillips and Christie studies could use verbal labelling and other forms of coding that did not rely on a specialised visual store. Of course, this raises the intriguing idea that if there is scope for some form of verbal coding for the pre-recency items, then there remains the possibility that subjects may readily retain a more detailed verbal code for the last items in the sequence, resulting in what is essentially a *verbal* recency effect. Thus the serial position curves for retention of a series of patterns (such as those used in these experiments) may reflect the operation of general-purpose resources plus the use of a specialised *verbal* rather than a specialised visual resource. This is a plausible explanation for the Phillips and Christie result. It is less likely (although not inconceivable) that this interpretation would apply to the less regular and more abstract patterns used by Broadbent and Broadbent.

Some more recent studies by Hitch and colleagues (Hitch & Walker, 1991) have explored visual recency effects using a rather different paradigm. In their experiments subjects were shown a series of letters, each letter appearing in a different colour in one of four positions along the top of a computer screen. Each letter disappeared before the next one was presented. After all of the letters had been shown, a probe item appeared in a box in the centre of the screen. For some of the trials, the probe was a colour patch, and the subject was required to point to the location of the item that was previously presented in that colour. For other trials, the probe comprised a letter shape shown in a neutral colour, and the subject had to point to the location where the letter appeared. Hitch and Walker then plotted the number of items whose location was correctly identified against the serial position of the item in the original presentation sequence. In order to undermine subjects' use of verbal coding, adult subjects were required to suppress articulation throughout presentation of the sequence. Under these conditions, for both colour and for letter shape there was a clear one-item recency effect very similar to that found by Phillips and Christie for sequences of matrix patterns. Of particular interest here is that the effect occurred even when subjects were ostensibly prevented, by articulatory suppression, from using verbal rehearsal. Moreover, Hitch and Walker found the same one-item recency effect in five-year-old children. In children of this age there is now a reasonable amount of evidence to suggest that they do not use verbal coding spontaneously (Hitch & Halliday, 1983; Hitch, Halliday, Schaafstal, & Schraagen, 1988).

These results are inconsistent with the suggestion that subjects use verbal codes in retention of series of visual patterns. Thus the recency effect in these experiments does at first glance appear to be based on some form of visual coding.

However, three caveats remain. The first of these stems from the reliance on a recency effect as a measure of visual short-term memory function. The second problem arises from the persistent possibility of verbal coding and from the assumption that articulatory suppression is a technique for suppressing the use of such verbal coding. A third problem is the suggestion by Phillips and Christie that the visual recency effect may reflect the operation of general purpose resources rather than a specifically visual short-term memory.

Dealing first with recency, it was clear from the discussion in Chapter 1 that recency effects cannot provide unequivocal support for the operation of a short-term memory system. You may recall for example that verbal recency does not correlate with digit span, suggesting that these two measures rely on the operation of different cognitive systems. Moreover recency has been demonstrated for sequences of events that were experienced over periods of weeks and months, and thus recency *per se* does not uniquely implicate short-term storage. In the visual domain we should be cautious about coming to the conclusion that a visual recency effect necessarily implicates a visual short-term memory system. One reason for caution is the persistent possibility that subjects are using verbal coding, and this is discussed shortly. Further, the study of recency in verbal short-term memory was based on the reasonable assumption that verbal temporary storage is inherently sequential in nature in the same way that speech is sequential. In this context, a recency effect makes some intuitive sense. However it is not clear whether a visual short-term storage system would have analogous properties. Many aspects of vision are inherently parallel rather than sequential in nature. Although we can sequentially scan different parts of a scene, this is a very different sequential process from the Phillips and Christie procedure where subjects were shown a sequence of unconnected discrete stimuli. Thus it makes more sense to suggest that the limitations on visual short-term storage may be in terms of pattern complexity, (e.g. Kosslyn, 1980) and how long that pattern can be retained (e.g. Kikuchi, 1987) rather than how many patterns can be stored. That is, Phillips and Christie may be right to suggest that visual short-term memory can store only a single pattern, but whether the number of patterns stored is the most crucial constraint on the system is a moot point.

To turn to the second caveat, Hitch and Walker's conclusions rest in part on the assumption that articulatory suppression stops subjects using letter names or colour names, or using verbal descriptions of the location of items on the screen. This same issue cropped up when discussing the Brandimonte and Gerbino studies in Chapter 2. There is certainly strong evidence that articulatory suppression inhibits subvocal rehearsal (for a detailed discussion see Chapter 4), but there is not convincing evidence that it prevents naming. Certainly in the Hitch and Walker studies and in the Brandimonte experiments, articulatory suppression appeared to make it less likely that subjects would use names for pictured objects. Thus although articulatory suppression does not make verbal coding impossible, it may make it a less likely strategy. A further effect of articulatory suppression of course stems from its effect on memory for the verbal codes. That is, it is certainly possible to name objects mentally while repeating an irrelevant word. However it is very difficult to retain the names of those objects in sequential order while suppressing articulation. Thus whether verbal codes are used or not may depend on the extent to which task demands make it useful to remember those verbal labels, or whether the task can be accomplished merely by identifying what the verbal label is for a depicted pattern or object without a memory requirement. It is however perfectly possible to retain a single verbal item while suppressing articulation (e.g. Murray, 1968). Therefore the one-item recency effect obtained in the Phillips and Christie studies and for the adults in the Hitch and Walker experiments could still be interpreted as memory for a verbal label associated with the recency item, rather than reflecting the capacity of a visual short-term memory system.

In the context of the third caveat, in a study by myself and colleagues (Logie, Zucco, & Baddeley, 1990), we attempted to tackle the argument about whether specialised or general-purpose resources underpin visual short-term storage function. We argued that an important aspect of the Phillips and Christie (1977a;b) experiments with interpolated mental arithmetic was that they took little account of the *nature* of the interpolated task. It is clear from the literature on mental arithmetic that it may involve general purpose resources, verbal short-term storage and/or visual imagery as well as accessing long-term memory (see e.g. Ashcraft, 1992; Dehaene, 1992; Hayes, 1973; Logie, Gilhooly, & Wynn, 1994; Widaman, Geary, Cormier, & Little, 1989). In view of the discussion in the previous paragraph the disruptive effects of arithmetic could be due to its demand on verbal resources, visual resources, or general-purpose resources, singly or in combination.

In the Logie et al. (1990) paper, we examined the link between mental arithmetic and visual short-term memory in more detail. In one experiment we presented subjects with single matrix patterns similar to those used in the Phillips and Christie studies, with half of the cells filled at random. Shortly after presentation of an individual pattern, subjects were shown the same pattern again, but with one of the previously filled cells changed to a blank cell. The subject's task was to point to the square that had been changed. However, as the trials progressed the total number of cells in the matrix gradually increased, although only one of the cells (chosen at random) was changed on any one trial. This was essentially a visual memory span procedure, with performance measured by the maximum number of cells in the matrix for which the subject could reliably identify a changed cell. The procedure was adapted from a technique reported by Wilson, Scott, and Power (1987), and examples of the stimuli are shown in Fig. 3.5. This procedure differed from that used by Phillips and Christie in that subjects had to remember only one pattern at a time. In avoiding a procedure that involved presenting a sequence of patterns, we were essentially finessing the interpretation of visual recency. Moreover by looking at patterns that increased in complexity this made it less likely that subjects could rely on verbal coding, and in so doing we attempted to provide converging evidence for a visual short-term memory system.

We chose two secondary tasks. The first of these involved simple mental arithmetic in which subjects heard a series of numbers to be added up. This was intended to explore further the use of mental arithmetic adopted in the Phillips and Christie studies. The other secondary task involved asking subjects to visualise a three by five square matrix. Subjects then heard a series of instructions to fill or to leave blank each of the cells of the imagined matrix. When presentation of these instructions was complete, the pattern of filled and unfilled squares in the visualised matrix comprised one of the digits between 0 and 9. The subject's task was to report which of the digits was represented in the pattern. An example of the number image task is shown in Fig. 3.6.

The logic of the experiment was that a secondary task that involved the use of the same cognitive resources as the visual span task would interfere substantially with visual span. In contrast a secondary task involving the use of different resources from those required for visual span should have very little if any disruptive effect. If only general-purpose resources are used to perform the visual span task, then there should be no such

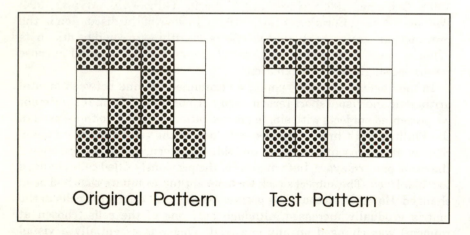

Original Pattern   Test Pattern

FIG. 3.5. Example of visual span stimuli used in Logie, Zucco, and Baddeley (1990).

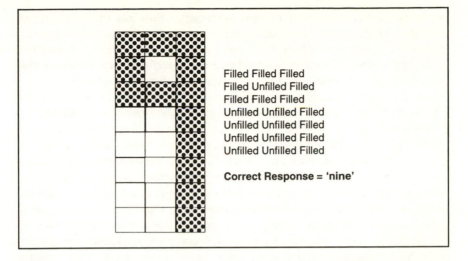

Filled Filled Filled
Filled Unfilled Filled
Filled Filled Filled
Unfilled Unfilled Filled
Unfilled Unfilled Filled
Unfilled Unfilled Filled
Unfilled Unfilled Filled

Correct Response = 'nine'

FIG. 3.6. Example of the number image task used by Logie, Zucco, and Baddeley (1990).

systematic relationship between the nature of the secondary task and the degree of disruption of visual span.

However, there remains the possibility that one of the secondary tasks is simply more difficult than the other, for example the "number matrix" task might be generally more difficult than the mental arithmetic task. If this were the case, we might expect that the visual span task would be disrupted more by the number matrix task solely on the grounds of the difficulty of performing two tasks together. In order to investigate this possibility we added a further primary task, namely letter span. Here, subjects saw a series of letters appearing on the screen, one at a time. After a brief delay the same series of letters was shown again, but with one of the letters changed. The subject's task was to detect which of the letters had been changed from the original series, and the number of letters in the series increased over trials.

If task difficulty is the most important factor we would expect that combining the two most difficult tasks would produce the poorest performance, regardless of the nature of those tasks. However, if specialised resources are employed on the basis of the nature of the cognitive processing required, then we would expect a rather different pattern. Specifically, the number matrix task should disrupt visual span more so than letter span, whereas the converse should hold for mental arithmetic.

The results of this experiment are shown in Fig. 3.7. From the figure, it is clear that there was a small but significant disruption of visual span performance by concurrent mental arithmetic. This result is congruent with the impairment by arithmetic of the single-item recency effect in the Phillips et al. studies. There was also a small and significant disruptive effect by the number matrix task on letter span performance. However, the most striking feature of the result was the dramatic differential disruption of visual span by concurrent visualising of a number matrix, coupled with an equally dramatic disruption of letter span by concurrent arithmetic.

We concluded from this study that perhaps there was a general processing load involved but that it was relatively small when compared with the differential disruption associated with the nature of the tasks that were combined. The results are highly consistent with the use of a specialised verbal short-term store for the letter span task and a specialised visual short-term store for the visual span task. The verbal store appears to be involved in both storage of a verbal sequence and in mental arithmetic. There is other evidence for the role of a verbal short-term store in both of these tasks (Dehaene, 1992; Logie, Gilhooly, & Wynn, 1994; Widaman et al, 1989. For a discussion see Chapter 4). Some form of visual store appears to be involved in visualising and in retaining the visually presented matrix patterns.

The case for a visual short-term storage system now seems to be somewhat stronger. The data described in this chapter are certainly

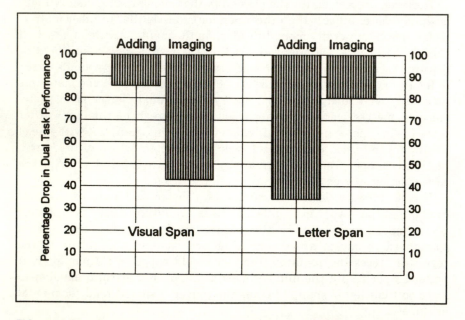

FIG. 3.7. Results from the Logie, Zucco, and Baddeley (1990) experiments.

consistent with the idea of such a specialised mechanism. They also hint at some of its characteristics. For example, the fact that subjects retain complex patterns less well than simple patterns suggests that the memory system involved is affected by pattern complexity.[1] This same memory system appears to use cognitive resources that overlap with those required to generate visual images from auditory input. It also seems to rely but only in part, on some general processing resource.

The case is by no means proven, and several puzzles remain, such as whether the system deals only with visual material, or with spatial information as well. Also, the relationship between visuo-spatial working memory and verbal working memory is not at all clear. In the next chapter I attempt to explore these issues.

NOTES

1. Complexity here is operationally defined in terms of the number of cells in the presented matrix, and it is recognised that further development would benefit from a more precise definition.

CHAPTER FOUR

Working Memory

In the United Kingdom, the study of short-term memory function over the last 20 years has been influenced to a great extent by the notion of working memory. Working memory refers to the temporary storage and manipulation of information. It is involved in information processing during the performance of a wide range of everyday tasks, as well as in laboratory studies of short-term storage. As I discussed in Chapter 1, working memory grew out of a dissatisfaction in the early 1970s with the idea of a single short-term storage and processing system, characterised most notably in the Atkinson and Shiffrin (1968) model. This led Baddeley and Hitch (1974) to propose a working memory which comprised a number of components. One component, the central executive, was proposed as the system responsible for reasoning, decision making, and coordinating the operation of subsidiary specialised "slave" systems. Two slave systems were proposed initially, namely the visuo-spatial sketch-pad, or VSSP, and the articulatory loop. The visuo-spatial sketch-pad was considered to be responsible for the temporary storage and manipulation of visuo-spatial material, while the articulatory loop provided a similar function for verbal material.

This scheme has remained broadly intact (Baddeley, 1986), although the characterisation of the components of working memory has become somewhat clearer, and the articulatory loop is now often referred to as the phonological loop. The component about which least is known is also the most complex, namely the central executive, although I discussed in

Chapter 1 some of the evidence that this system plays a role in coordinating dual-task performance (Baddeley, Bressi, Della Sala, Logie, & Spinnler, 1991; Baddeley, Logie, Bressi, Della Sala, & Spinnler, 1986). However, much remains to be explored.

In contrast, the concept of the phonological loop has become significantly more sophisticated (Baddeley & Logie, 1992; Salamé & Baddeley, 1982, 1989). In this chapter, I shall explore the possibilities of drawing analogies between the characteristics of the phonological loop, and those of the visuo-spatial sketch-pad. Therefore, before going on to describe the literature on the VSSP, it would be useful at this stage to describe the basic findings and phenomena associated with the phonological loop model, and how these findings led to its theoretical development. These phenomena are often thought of as the rudiments of verbal short-term memory, and collectively they provide converging evidence for the characteristics of the phonological loop.

THE PHONOLOGICAL LOOP
The Phonological Similarity Effect

This is probably one of the best known phenomena associated with verbal short-term memory, and it was discussed briefly in Chapter 1 as one source of evidence for a distinction between short-term and long-term memory. Specifically it refers to the fact that recall of a series of words or letters is more difficult when the words or letters for recall sound alike. Thus a series such as "Mat, Cat, Fat, Rat, Hat, Chat" is rather more difficult to recall in its original order than is a sequence such as "Bus, Clock, Spoon, Fish, Grate, Men". This effect, known as the phonological similarity effect or as the acoustic similarity effect, has been widely replicated with different sets of materials (e.g. Baddeley, 1966a; Conrad, 1964), and appears for verbal materials that the subject is asked to read as well as for materials that are heard. That is, when subjects are asked to read and remember a verbal sequence they appear to translate the visually presented material into a phonologically based code for temporary storage. When a word is heard it appears to be directly encoded phonologically.

Irrelevant Speech

Verbal serial recall also is disrupted by the concurrent presentation of irrelevant speech. This disruptive effect is even greater when the irrelevant speech comprises words that are phonologically similar to the words for recall. Thus recall of a list of visually presented digits is most impaired by irrelevant speech comprising words that sound like digits "TUN, WOO,

TEE, SORE, THRIVE" and so on. The general disruptive effect of irrelevant speech has also been referred to as the unattended speech effect (Salamé & Baddeley, 1982).

Word Length Effect

A further phenomenon in verbal serial recall is that sequences of long words such as "University, Aluminium, Hippopotamus, Mississippi, Refrigerator" can be recalled rather less well than sequences of short words such as "Pen, Book, Chair, Greece, Nail". This word length effect seems to apply to the length of time required to pronounce the words rather than the number of syllables or letters they contain. Thus sequences of words that can be pronounced fairly rapidly for example "Cricket, Bishop, Parrot" can be retained in sequence rather more readily than can words that take a relatively longer time to pronounce such as "Friday, Typhoon", (Baddeley, Thomson, & Buchanan, 1975).

Articulatory Suppression

Finally, retaining a verbal sequence is dramatically impaired when subjects are simultaneously required to repeat aloud an irrelevant speech sound such as "the, the, the" or "hiya, hiya, hiya" (Levy, 1971, 1975; Murray, 1965, 1968). This technique, known as articulatory suppression, also removes the effect of word length for visual and auditory presentation, and removes the phonological similarity effect but only when the list for recall is presented visually (Baddeley, Lewis, & Vallar, 1984).

Interpreting the Phenomena

This set of findings has been interpreted in terms of a model of the phonological loop comprising two components; a passive phonological store and an articulatory rehearsal process. A diagram of the model in its current form is shown in Fig. 4.1.

According to this model, information that the subject hears goes directly into the phonological store and is maintained in the store by means of subvocal, articulatory-based rehearsal. Information that the subject reads is transferred into the phonological store via articulatory rehearsal.

The model accounts for the effects of articulatory suppression by suggesting that the technique blocks the use of articulatory rehearsal, thereby undermining an important facility for retention. The phonological similarity effect arises because items contained within the phonological store will become confused when they are phonologically similar to one another. As verbal sequences are held in this store whether they are heard

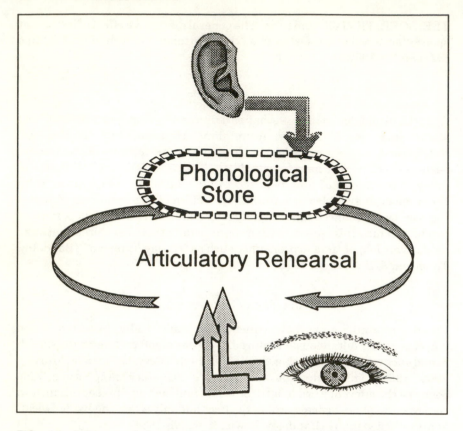

FIG. 4.1. A diagram of phonological loop derived from Baddeley (1986).

or read, the phonological similarity effect appears for both visually presented and auditorily presented material. With articulatory suppression, visually presented material cannot be transferred into the phonological store and the phonological similarity effect disappears. As auditory presentation results in direct input into the phonological store, the potential for phonological confusion remains even with articulatory suppression.

The effect of irrelevant speech arises from the fact that heard speech directly accesses the phonological store, thereby disrupting its current contents.

The word length effect is interpreted as reflecting the operation of subvocal rehearsal. Words that take a longer time to say are more difficult to rehearse, and therefore will be less well retained. Words are rehearsed whether they are heard or read, and therefore the word length effect appears for both visual and auditory presentation. Because articulatory suppression blocks the operation of this function it removes the potential for rehearsing words of different length, and the word length effect disappears. Moreover, the number of items that subjects can retain appears to depend on their speaking rate. For example Hulme, Thomson, Muir, and Lawrence (1984) measured speech rate and verbal memory span in children of different ages. They discovered that the speed at which children can speak increases with their age, and that this increase in speech rate was closely related to an increase with age in short-term verbal memory span.

The strength of the phonological loop model is that with a very simple organisation and few assumptions, it can cope with a number of diverse laboratory findings. In addition, the utility of the model is not restricted to accounting for these specific laboratory phenomena. For example the mean digit span for normal adults using different languages depends on the length of time it takes to pronounce the words for digits in those languages. Thus digit span in Welsh is lower than is digit span in English because the Welsh digit words take longer to say than do the English equivalents (Ellis & Hennelley, 1980). The converse is true for a comparison between Chinese and English (Hoosain & Salili, 1988; Stigler, Lee, & Stevenson, 1986). That is, for several dialects of Chinese the words for digits take less time to say than do the English words for digits, and digit span in Chinese is higher as a result. Similar correlations between pronunciation time and digit span have been reported in comparisons of English with Italian, Arabic, Hebrew, and a number of other languages (see e.g. Della Sala & Logie, 1993; Naveh-Benjamin & Ayres, 1986). The phonological loop also appears to be involved in normal counting (Logie & Baddeley, 1987), in mental arithmetic (Logie, Gilhooly & Wynn, 1994; Dehaene, 1992), in aspects of reading (Baddeley & Lewis, 1981), language comprehension (McCarthy & Warrington, 1987; Shallice, 1988, p.63; Vallar & Baddeley, 1984, 1987), in children's acquisition of language (Gathercole & Baddeley, 1989; 1990), and in adult acquisition of foreign language vocabulary (Baddeley, Papagno, & Vallar, 1988). For more detailed reviews of literature on the phonological loop, see Baddeley (1986) or Baddeley and Logie (1992).

There is also evidence for the phonological loop derived from studies of neuropsychological patients. A number of patients with severe short-term verbal memory deficits have been described who exhibit patterns of deficit and sparing in the phenomena described earlier (for reviews see Caplan & Waters, 1990; Della Sala & Logie, 1993). On the whole their patterns of deficit are consistent with damage to the phonological storage component of the loop. For example patient P.V. (Basso et al, 1982; Vallar & Baddeley, 1984) has an auditory digit span of just two items, and she fails to show word length or phonological similarity effects with visual presentation.

With auditory presentation she does show a phonological similarity effect, but does not show a word length effect. These data are interpreted by suggesting that P.V. has damage to the phonological loop. However with heard material, access to this store is direct, and she has no choice but to rely on the damaged system. Although the normal pattern of findings does not appear spontaneously, memory span for visually presented items is rather higher than it is for auditory presentation. One suggestion with these kinds of patients is that for the visually presented material they are relying on some form of visual store, and in the next section of this chapter I shall discuss the evidence from studies of normal subjects for the use of such a store in the retention of visually presented verbal material.

The phonological loop is not without its critics, and a number of complications have arisen. Thus for example, Longoni, Richardson, and Aiello (1993) have shown that retention of verbal sequences in a phono-logical form is not necessarily dependent on articulatory rehearsal. Specifically, they found that in normal subjects, the phonological similarity effect with auditory presentation survived a delay of 10 seconds between presentation and recall even when this delay was filled with articulatory suppression. Moreover Bishop and Robson (1989) reported that children who have been unable to speak from birth (congenital anarthrics) neverthe-less show word length effects in serial verbal recall tasks. This kind of evidence points to the idea that rehearsal can be phonologically based and that word length effects can arise from the use of phonological coding. For these kinds of reasons, the original term "articulatory loop" is sometimes replaced by the term "phonological loop" (Baddeley & Logie, 1992). Waters, Rochon, and Caplan (1992) have also suggested that some of the phenomena associated with serial verbal recall might arise from the mechanisms responsible for planning speech prior to production of articulation.

An interesting aspect of this evidence for the role of phonological coding is that it does not undermine the conclusion that word length effects can result from the use of subvocal articulation even if it is not the only source of the effect (Martin, 1987; see also Monsell, 1987). As mooted in Chapter 2, subjects can be strategic in their approach to experimental tasks and some normal subjects spontaneously fail to show word length and phonological similarity effects (Della Sala et al, 1991; Logie et al, submitted). This is accounted for largely by whether or not they have attempted to use subvocal rehearsal when retaining the word list for recall. For example one subject in the Della Sala et al. study who failed to show the standard effects had a word span of nine items and reported spontaneously using semantic associates and imagery mnemonics to perform the task. When specifically instructed to use subvocal rehearsal the effects of phonological similarity and word length appeared in his data pattern. A similar failure to show the phonological similarity effect with visual presentation for normal adults was reported by Hanley, Young, and Pearson (1991). This is an intriguing debate, but I shall avoid the temptation to discuss it in detail here (see e.g. Logie et al, submitted; Logie, in press). Nevertheless, the notion that some aspects of working memory might be involved in planning response output is a theme that I shall return to later in the book.

VISUO-SPATIAL WORKING MEMORY

Clearly extensive research effort has been directed towards the study of phonological and articulatory components of working memory. The visuo-spatial component of working memory has received much less attention, although there has been considerably more than a flurry of activity in this area over the last few years.

In the working memory literature, visuo-spatial working memory was originally referred to as the visuo-spatial sketch pad. As I mentioned in Chapter 1, this term was later changed to the visuo-spatial scratch pad. This modified term was thought to convey less of an impression of a system that dealt only with pictorial material, and more of a system that could deal with all visuo-spatial material, for example word shape and letter shape (Baddeley, 1986). In practice, the two names are used interchangeably in the literature, or the ambiguity is avoided by using the abbreviation VSSP. As I have hinted already, the concept of a single visuo-spatial working memory system may be rather simplistic in the face of the data collated thus far, and I shall continue to use the more generic term visuo-spatial working memory and the abbreviation VSWM when referring to those functions of working memory that store and process visual and spatial information.

Basic Requirements for Visuo-spatial Working Memory

The model for the phonological loop was based on the accumulation of evidence from a variety of sources. Such a model provided a framework within which to ask theoretically derived questions that could be explored experimentally both with normal subjects and with neurological patients. Until recently, the lack of a substantive body of research on VSWM has been accompanied by a lack of an explicit model or framework for studying visuo-spatial working memory. In other words we need some basis from which to generate and test hypotheses, as well as to provide accounts for patterns of data. In the main, exploration has been largely data driven. A separate, specialised visuo-spatial working memory system has been assumed, and experiments have been designed to explore what might be its characteristics. However, some of the basic assumptions underlying these studies tend not to be made explicit.

To tackle these issues I should like to consider a number of basic functions that would be required of any temporary memory system, and will then go on to see how the available data on VSWM fit with these basic requirements.

Any temporary memory system ought to have some means by which information gets into such a memory system from the senses or from longer-term storage. Further, given that information is held on a temporary basis, the system must be subject to a process by which information may be lost over time, either through decay of the memory trace or by interference from new material displacing what is already in the system. Such a system should also have some means to extend the period of retention should this be necessary. Finally, given that it is a system that purports to store or manipulate visual and/or spatial material, the memory codes involved should have some relationship with the characteristics of the visual and spatial material with which the system has to deal.

Given that most of these characteristics are basic requirements of any temporary memory system, it is not surprising that they are similar to some of the basic characteristics incorporated into the model of the phonological loop. Both in its original concept (Baddeley & Hitch, 1974) and in more recent discussions (Baddeley, 1986, 1990; Hanley et al., 1991; Logie, 1989, 1991; Morris, 1987) visuo-spatial working memory has been thought of as complementary to the phonological loop. This view has been supported by an increasing body of data. Thus my approach will be to explore the extent to which the model of the phonological loop might act as a framework for a model of visuo-spatial working memory.

A Possible Cognitive Architecture

One of the recurring themes in the study of the articulatory or phonological loop was that there appeared to be an overlap between the speech system (processing of speech and speech output) and verbal short-term storage, suggested for example by the effects of phonological similarity and of word length, along with the role of phonology and articulation. In the visuo-spatial domain a sensible question appears to be whether there is an overlap between the visual-perceptual system and visuo-spatial short-term storage. I shall discuss this question in three ways—first by exploring whether *visual* similarity among stimuli for retention results in confusions in memory. If the system under scrutiny relies on visual codes then we should expect to find evidence of visual confusions in memory for stimuli that are visually similar to one another. A second approach will be to study the relationship between retention of visual information and retention of spatial information. Specifically, are visual information and spatial information dealt with in similar ways and by the same system, or do they involve two quite separate systems? Third and finally, there is the broader issue of the link between visual short-term storage and visual imagery. I have already discussed this to some extent in Chapters 2 and 3, but will return to the issue later in this chapter, specifically in the context of working memory.

Is There a Visual Similarity Effect?

Do confusions arise in memory for visually similar materials? There is certainly evidence that visual confusions occur when subjects attempt to remember visually presented letters or characters that are visually similar to one another. Hue and Ericsson (1988) reported visual similarity effects in immediate recall of unfamiliar Chinese characters. Wolford and Hollingsworth (1974) reported visual confusion errors in the recall of verbal stimuli that were presented visually, but very briefly.

In a review paper, Frick (1988) argued that images in visual short-term memory are both unparsed and uncategorised. So, for example, Frick reports that when visual confusion errors occur in retention of letters there appears to be independent degradation of parts of the letter. Thus the letter "P" might be mistakenly recalled as an "R". Also, when subjects are asked to retain visually presented numbers, the font in which the number is printed appears to be associated with the incidence of visual confusions rather than the number itself. For example, a square block character for the digit "9" is mistakenly recalled as an "8" more often than if the digit "9" is displayed as a continuous curve (See Fig. 4.2). Despite these confusions, subjects have no difficulty identifying the digits presented in different fonts. This supports the idea that the visual confusions arise because of the nature of the code stored in temporary visual memory, rather than because of difficulties in perceiving the presented digits.

Some as yet unpublished data of our own (Logie, Della Sala, & Baddeley, in preparation) provide evidence for visual similarity effects in the recall of letter case. Letters were chosen where the upper and lower case versions were visually similar, for example Kk, Cc, Pp, Ss, or were visually different, for example Gg, Bb, Rr, Qq. Therefore, subjects might see a sequence such as "K C P s" or "g B r Q" and would then be asked to write down the sequence in the correct order, and with the correct case for each letter. When subjects had to perform this task and suppress articulation at the same time, they had more difficulty recalling the case of presentation of the letters drawn from the set where the upper and lower case versions of the letters were visually similar. As I discussed earlier, articulatory suppression is thought to inhibit the use of subvocalisation, and in the case of letter stimuli it is

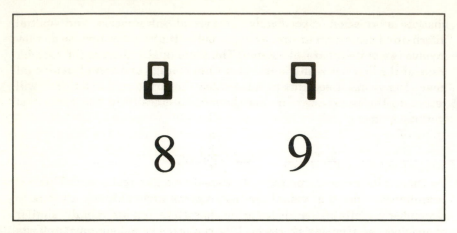

FIG. 4.2. Examples of block and curved fonts used for displaying the digits 8 and 9, derived from Frick (1988).

thought to inhibit the use of letter names for retention. Thus with articulatory suppression subjects are more likely to rely on some form of visual code for the letters. This visual similarity effect was robust and was replicated in a series of such experiments. However in one of these experiments, to our chagrin, the effect was much reduced. We subsequently discovered that this was due to the use of a different computer monitor in the experiment, and that this monitor used a different font for presenting the letters. Thus an upper case/lower case pair that we had previously classified as visually dissimilar actually looked visually similar on the screen. This provided serendipitous support for the findings in our other experiments. In the main experiments there was in addition a visual similarity effect when subjects were not suppressing articulation, suggesting that even when phonological or articulatory codes for the letters are potentially available, they may not necessarily be used to discriminate between upper and lower case versions of the letter. Note that these data are consistent with the suggestion of a specialised visuo-spatial temporary store, but they leave open the question as to whether information in that store is unparsed and uncategorised.

Further evidence has come from cognitive developmental patterns in children. Hitch, Halliday, Schaafstal, and Schraagen (1988) reported that young children show visual confusion errors in recognition memory for a series of pictures. Thus retention of pictures that are visually similar to one another such as a pen, a rake, and a brush is more difficult for five-year-old children than is retention of a series comprising items that are visually distinct such as a ball, a pen, and a pig. With older children Hitch, Woodin, and Baker (1989) have shown that the visual similarity effect tends to disappear except when the children are required to suppress articulation. Hitch and his colleagues argued that young children rely on visual codes because their use of verbal codes (object names), and their use of subvocal rehearsal are not yet fully developed. Older children can use both visual codes and verbal codes, but tend to rely on the latter unless prevented (or discouraged) from doing so by articulatory suppression.

In the experiments by Hitch and Walker (1991) described in Chapter 3, there were also significant visual similarity effects based on the shape of the letters for recall. This appeared both for five-year-old children and for normal adults under articulatory suppression.

These data suggest that there appears to be a visual similarity effect in retention by normal adults and young normal children of visually presented material. This supports the idea of a temporary memory system that relies on visual codes. However, except in the case of young children, the effect only appears in particular circumstances such as under articulatory suppression or with material that is very difficult to name. It has not been studied nor replicated as widely as has the phonological similarity effect in immediate serial verbal recall. It appears then that although visual similarity effects appear, they are relatively weak, and they are often undermined by the strong tendency in normal adults to use verbal codes.

Visual or Spatial?

You may recall from Chapter 3 that a fruitful approach to the study of visual short-term memory stemmed from the work of Brooks (1967; 1968), and from subsequent studies by Baddeley, Grant, Wight, and Thomson (1975). Just to serve as a reminder, Baddeley et al. found that recall of the Brooks matrix patterns (see Fig. 3.2, p.46) was disrupted by concurrent tracking of a moving target, but that concurrent tracking had no effect on recall of the verbal sequences. In a follow-up study, Baddeley and Lieberman (1980) showed that the Brooks matrix task was also disrupted by a tracking task that was spatial but not visual. In this case subjects were blindfolded (to remove any visual input), and had to follow a moving pendulum with a flashlight. They were given auditory feedback to indicate whether or not the flashlight was accurately following the movement of the pendulum.

Retention of the matrix was not affected by a concurrent, purely visual task. Baddeley and Lieberman further demonstrated that concurrent tracking disrupted the use of a spatial mnemonic technique known as the method of loci. Tracking had a much weaker effect on the use of a visual mnemonic technique based on visual images of number–word rhyming pairs, a technique known as the pegword mnemonic (see Paivio, 1971 for a discussion of mnemonic techniques).

This pattern of results led Baddeley and Lieberman to suggest that visuo-spatial working memory did indeed comprise a system that was involved in visuo-spatial retention, in visuo-spatial perception, and in motor control. They also concluded that the system was most likely to be a spatial system rather than a purely visual, or a visuo-spatial system. It was left unclear as to the nature of the system that would retain more visually based material.

In a series of studies of my own (Logie, 1986), I argued that the lack of disruption by a concurrent visual task may have arisen from the spatial nature of the Brooks matrix task and of the method of loci, rather than reflecting the characteristics of the functional system involved in performing the task. If subjects are required to perform a *visual* imagery rather than a *spatial* imagery task, then can performance be disrupted by a concurrent visual task?

The experiments involved subjects retaining a series of words, either by means of the one-bun pegword mnemonic or by means of verbal rote rehearsal. The pegword mnemonic is generally considered to rely on visual imagery for its success in enhancing verbal recall (e.g. Paivio, 1971), and the visual nature of this task was assumed by Baddeley and Lieberman.

These two forms of the memory task (pegword or rote rehearsal) were combined with presentation of irrelevant visual patterns. You may recall from the discussion of the phonological loop that irrelevant speech seemed to have direct access to the phonological short-term store, causing disruption of its contents, and this was the basis for choosing irrelevant visual patterns. I have argued earlier that one of the basic requirements of a visual short-term memory system is that visually presented stimuli should have ready access to such a system. If visual imagery and visual perception involve overlapping cognitive functions, then visual input of irrelevant material should have some disruptive effect on tasks that rely on the use of visual imagery. When presented with the irrelevant visual patterns, subjects were asked to try to ignore the patterns as far as possible, but without closing their eyes or looking away, and to concentrate on remembering the list of words.

The results were clear. When subjects were asked to use the visual mnemonic, concurrent irrelevant patterns disrupted recall. Concurrent pictures had no effect on recall following rote rehearsal. It is possible that the lack of an effect on rote rehearsal was due to the relatively low level of recall with this strategy even without the presence of irrelevant material. This possible alternative interpretation was tested by replacing the irrelevant visual patterns with irrelevant speech. If the initial set of results was due to a floor effect in the rote rehearsal condition, then irrelevant speech should not cause performance to drop any lower than that achieved without the irrelevant material. However when the memory task was combined with irrelevant speech, rote rehearsal was significantly disrupted while use of the visual imagery mnemonic was largely unimpaired. This then rules out an interpretation based on a possible floor effect. This cross-over interaction is illustrated in Fig. 4.3.

There was one major difficulty with the irrelevant pictures effect, namely that by using pictures it is possible that some form of semantic activation is the basis for the interference. That is, the use of mnemonics involves the semantic features of the material being remembered in order to create a coherent visual image as an aid to later recall. A series of pictures of common objects may also activate the semantic system. Rote rehearsal is less likely to involve semantic coding and this could account for its insensitivity to disruption from irrelevant, but meaningful, visual stimuli.

With respect to the problem of possible semantic intereference, further experiments in the Logie (1986) paper showed similar selective interference effects with square matrix patterns and with coloured squares rather than pictures. The effect for matrix patterns was equivalent to that found for the irrelevant pictures. The selective disruption by coloured squares was present but slight. Both findings undermine an account of the interference effects in terms of semantic interference.

In some very recent studies, Quinn and McConnell (1994) have demonstrated a selective irrelevant visual input effect using a continuously

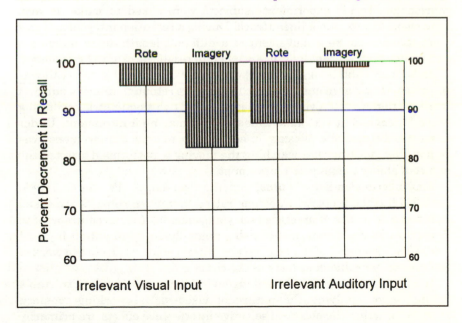

FIG. 4.3. Results from the Logie (1986) studies.

changing dot pattern as the irrelevant visual stimulus. As in the Logie (1986) studies, Quinn and McConnell asked subjects to use a visual imagery mnemonic or rote rehearsal. The irrelevant visual input comprised a display of numerous small squares which randomly turned black or white continuously. They found a very clear disruptive effect of this material on use of the mnemonic, but no dual task impairment of rote rehearsal. Like the matrix patterns in my own studies the material was abstract, and the interference effect is unlikely to be due to semantic interference.

Matthews (1983) reported analogous interference effects in subjects' retention of high- and low-imagery word lists. Mixed lists (high- and low-imagery) of words were presented auditorily while subjects were either asked to perform a shape-matching task or to perform a counting task. After presentation, subjects were asked to recall the word lists. The usual memory advantage for high-imagery words was found in the counting condition, but not in the shape-matching condition. Matthews interpreted this differential disruption of memory for the high-imagery words as reflecting the communal use of a visual imagery based system for dealing both with visually presented shapes and with retention of high-imagery words.

Interference effects have also been found in the spatial domain. Johnson (1982) investigated the effects of a visual interference task on memory for movements. In his experiments subjects were asked to make an arm movement to a stop on a linear track. During a retention interval subjects were asked to make a movement of a different length, or to imagine a movement of a different length, and then to recall the original movement. With both real and imagined interpolated movements subjects' recall was impaired. However in one condition, during the retention interval subjects were asked to watch a visual display showing two asymmetric oscillating wave forms, and at the same time were to imagine a movement. Under these conditions, the biasing effect of the imagined movement was removed, suggesting that watching the moving wave forms disrupted the subjects' ability to imagine a movement.

Smyth and Pendleton (1989; Smyth, Pearson, & Pendleton, 1988) provided further support by demonstrating that when subjects are asked to retain a sequence of presented body movements, then a requirement to simply watch other movements being made during a retention interval interferes with recall of the original sequence. I shall return to the work of Smyth and her colleagues later in the chapter.

In sum, some form of irrelevant visual input appears to offer a tractable technique for studying the nature of visuo-spatial working memory. However whether the observed selective interference effects are primarily visual or primarily spatial remains an open question as interference with variants of this technique has been shown for both ostensibly visual and ostensibly spatial tasks. Therefore data from this technique alone are not sufficient, and we have to look for other sources of evidence that might help settle the putative visual versus spatial distinction.

Nevertheless, taken together the studies described earlier and experiments previously discussed are consistent with a temporary storage system for spatial information that also appears to be involved in movement tasks such as tracking. Moreover, there seems to be support for a system that is involved in generating and/or retaining visual images, and which has some role in retaining and in processing visual input. However, the unresolved issue is whether there is a single system that deals with both visual and spatial information, or whether some further fractionation of the system is required. Clearly any theory based on the notion of a single system would have to account for the role of movement and for the link with visual input as well as for the temporary storage functions. This seems an apposite point at which to tackle the issue more directly.

A Case for Fractionation

The neuropsychological evidence discussed in Chapter 1, for a dissociation between short-term and long-term memory, gained considerable momentum from the use of the double dissociation technique (contrasting but complementary patterns of deficits in patients). Similar neuropsychological dissociations have been used in developing and fractionating the phonological loop (Vallar & Baddeley, 1984). The data from Brooks (1967; 1968), Logie (1986), and Baddeley and his colleagues (e.g. Baddeley et al., 1975b; Baddeley & Lieberman, 1980) illustrate the use of an experimental (rather than a neuropsychological) double dissociation. In this case the dissociation is between verbal short-term memory and visuo-spatial short-term memory, respectively comprising two parishes of the diocese of working memory. Data from neuropsychological patients can also be used to dissociate verbal and visuo-spatial short-term memory. This comes from reports of patients with verbal short-term memory deficits, and contrasting patients who appear to have visual and/or spatial short-term memory deficits (De Renzi & Nichelli, 1975; Farah, Hammond, Levine, & Calvanio, 1988; Hanley et al., 1991). A fuller discussion of the neuropsychological data will be given in Chapter 5.

Returning to the data on healthy adults, the studies by Baddeley et al. (1975), Baddeley and Lieberman (1980), by Johnson (1982) and by Smyth and colleagues (1988; 1989) supported the idea that perceptuo-motor performance did seem to require overlapping resources with retention of spatial information. However the nature of the spatial information and the way in which it differs from visual information is really rather vague in the published literature. One way in which to think of the term "spatial" is as a reference to the location of items in space and the geometric relationships between those items. Visual information might then refer to properties of those items such as their shape, colour, and brightness. Another way in which to use the term "spatial" might be to refer to movement through space, for example scanning or moving from one item to another. A visual representation in working memory might involve retention of static visual arrays which incorporate geometric properties of the layout of objects or the relationship of the parts of a single object to one another. In this sense, to retain a purely visual representation of a scene there need be no distinction between an array of several objects and a visual display of a single object which has a number of components, in a form close to Marr's 2½-D sketch (Marr, 1982). The distinction is only required when we wish to identify objects in the scene in addition to retaining their visual form and their location in space relative to other objects in the scene.

Other interpretations of the term "spatial" may be possible in addition to these, and in the working memory literature at least, the assumed interpretation tends not to be made explicit. This ambiguity in the use of the term "spatial" tends to undermine its utility. One could be very pragmatic and define spatial as referring to a particular meaning of the word, or one could ignore the term altogether and use a less ambiguous vocabulary. In practice it is difficult to avoid the use of the term given its widespread, if equivocal, use in the literature and I lean towards the pragmatic approach. Of course this opens another can of worms, because it is extremely difficult to come up with a concise definition. My own inclination when using the term spatial is to refer to a representation that involves movement in its broad sense, to incorporate imagined movement as well as physical movement. This movement could be in the form of scanning a visual array (via perception or scanning a mental image), or movement to a target in the array (with or without visual input), or movement of objects in an array. It could also involve building up a representation of the geometric relationships between objects by scanning from one to another or moving from one to another. This is a loose description rather than a definition, and it may be that there are better ways of describing the concept behind this description. However this particular use of the term "spatial" is by no means idiosyncratic, as it does map onto at least some of the assumptions that are implicit in much of the working memory literature. The debate becomes more salient if one dips more than a toe into the literature on representation of space or on the neuropsychology of spatial representation. I shall discuss some of the relevant neuropsychological literature in Chapter 5. Some of the literature on normal spatial processing and representation I discuss in this chapter.

One key element of a spatial representation on which most people would agree is that it need not involve any form of visual perceptual input. Thus for example, the relative physical location of objects can be determined by hearing, by touch, or by arm movement, as well as vision, and few people would dispute that the blind can have spatial representations (e.g. Cornoldi, Cortesi, & Preti, 1991; Kerr, 1983; Millar, 1990). In each of these cases, movement is of course required to build up representations of the relative locations of objects in space. Whether some form of covert movement or imagined movement is required to maintain the representation of those locations, and to process the locational information is a topic that will be a major focus for the last chapter in this book.

In the meantime, when discussing the topic, I shall try to make clear the concepts and the assumptions adopted by the differing researchers cited. However some of the reasons for preferring to incorporate movement into the concept of a "spatial representation" should become clear in the following discussion of temporary memory for movements.

The Role of Movement

Temporary memory for movements has been examined systematically in a series of studies by Mary Smyth and her colleagues. In one set of studies, Smyth, Pearson, and Pendleton (1988) asked subjects to watch an experimenter perform a sequence of simple movements such as a forward bend of the head followed by the left arm raised above the head, a step forward onto the right leg, and so on. After presentation of the movement sequence, subjects were required to reproduce the movements in the order of presentation. Smyth et al. reported that subjects could recall a mean of 4.33 movements in sequential order. This was compared with mean verbal spans of 5.12 for these same subjects. Subjects were then asked to perform the movement span and verbal span tasks concurrently with articulatory suppression, or hand tapping to four switches arranged on a square board, or repeated arm movements. The arm movements involved touching the top of the head with both hands, followed by touching the shoulders, followed by touching the hips, and then returning to the head and repeating the sequence. Smyth et al. reported that the repeated arm movement during presentation impaired recall of the movement sequence but not of the verbal sequence. Articulatory suppression appeared to disrupt memory for the movement sequence as well as for the verbal sequence. Tapping four switches in a square had no effect on recall of the movement sequence.

However in Experiments 3 and 5 Smyth et al. asked subjects to retain a sequence of locations. This involved a task often referred to as "Corsi blocks" (De Renzi & Nichelli, 1975) where the experimenter points to a sequence of blocks chosen from a set of nine blocks arranged randomly on a board. The subjects' task is to recall the sequence of blocks indicated. Performance on the Corsi blocks task was not disrupted by "arm movement suppression", but was disrupted by tapping a square pattern of four switches. These data point to a distinction between body movements and movements to specified target locations. The distinction was reinforced by later studies which contrasted Corsi block span with memory for series of hand configurations (Smyth & Pendleton, 1989). These results, together with the evidence discussed earlier, lend added sustenance to the idea that a spatial/movement component of working memory is linked to the planning and control of movement to targets in space.

The role of movement has also been studied by Gerry Quinn in a series of experiments, combining unseen arm movements with the Brooks (1968) matrix task. In the Quinn and Ralston (1986) experiments, subjects had to move their arms around a square matrix taped to the table. The matrix on the table and the subject's arm were covered, and movements had to be completed without the subject being able to see their arm. This ensured that the concurrent movement task did not involve any visual processing. Quinn and Ralston compared the effects of unseen arm movements that were either compatible with the matrix pattern, or were incompatible. For example, say that the Brooks task involved a series of instructions such as "In the starting square put a 1, in the next square to the right put a 2, in the next square down put a 3" and so on. Compatible concurrent movement would comprise an arm movement to the right, followed by an arm movement down. Incompatible arm movement involved tracing out a boustrepedal pattern, where the arm moved to the right along the top row of the matrix, then down to the next row, moving to the left along that row and so on.

Quinn and Ralston found that incompatible movement disrupted recall of the Brooks matrix material, whereas compatible movement did not. They followed up this experiment with a "passive movement" condition where the experimenter held the subject's arm and moved it for them. Even under these conditions, there was a disruptive effect of passive incompatible movement. This finding suggested that the disruption was not due to a general attentional deficit. However, it was unfortunate that Quinn and Ralston did not include a verbal control condition involving the Brooks verbal material. It would have been nice to have demonstrated that retention of the verbal material was insensitive to disruption by movement, as even with passive movement subjects may covertly monitor the movement of their hands.

Quinn (1988) carried out the study just described, combining the Brooks matrix and Brooks verbal material with either arm movement or with brightness judgement. As before, concurrent movement interfered with the Brooks matrix task. However, the brightness judgement task also interfered with recall of the matrix patterns. The level of interference was not as substantial as that associated with arm movement, but the fact that brightness judgements had any effect at all is in contrast to the complete lack of an effect reported by Baddeley and Lieberman (1980).

Movement and brightness judgement also had equally disruptive, but small effects on recall of the Brooks verbal material. Moreover, Quinn (1988; 1991) also demonstrated that the disruptive effects on either of the Brooks tasks appeared only if the secondary tasks were performed during encoding of the material. No disruption occurred in dual task performance during a retention interval.

In combination, these results are pointing to some general processing load involved in combining these kinds of tasks. They also suggest that any disruption, whether it is due to specifically spatial interference or due to a more general cognitive load, occurs during encoding and not during temporary retention. This is a crucial point, because the data from the dual task studies involving the Brooks material (verbal or spatial) could be interpreted in terms of some general processing function; a function that deals with visuo-spatial temporary storage only as part of its cognitive remit.

The Role of General-purpose Resources

Some further insight into the problem just discussed might be gained by looking more closely at the assumptions underlying the adopted tasks. One of the assumptions is that the Brooks matrix task relies primarily on visuo-spatial processing and visuo-spatial resources, whereas the verbal version of the task relies primarily on verbal resources. The single and double dissociations reported in the literature (Baddeley & Lieberman, 1980; Brooks, 1968; Logie, Zucco, & Baddeley, 1990; Quinn, 1988, 1991; Quinn & Ralston, 1986) go some considerable way towards supporting the use of different cognitive resources for each of the Brooks tasks. What is missing is any direct test of the general processing load associated with performance of these tasks.

In practice, researchers equate the levels of recall performance on the verbal and matrix versions of the Brooks tasks by adjusting the number of sentences presented on each trial. For example, in the Logie et al. (1990) study, the matrix task involved six sentences, while the verbal task involved only four thereby resulting in control levels of performance of 92% and 88% respectively. In pilot studies where the number of sentences in each task is the same, recall performance for the verbal task is generally poorer than it is for the matrix task. The *explicit* assumption has been that the verbal task is on the whole the more difficult of the two, and hence uses more general-purpose resources in addition to its load on specifically verbal resources (Brooks, 1968). By equating levels of performance, one *implicit* assumption is that this also equates cognitive load.

These assumptions are pragmatically useful for designing experiments, but may not be theoretically secure. Let us assume, for example, that the verbal version of the task places heavy demands on the phonological loop, and that the matrix task places heavy demands on a specialised visuo-spatial system. Given this scenario the different levels of performance achieved for verbal and for spatial processing may reflect cognitive loads on two quite different systems. An assumption that follows from this is that the performance indicators for the two different tasks are directly comparable, but it is a matter of debate as to whether a 50% level of recall performance on the verbal task is necessarily equivalent to a 50% level of recall on the matrix task. We can only be confident about comparability if a single cognitive system underlies the performance of both tasks, and if the performance indicators operate on the same linear scale. Given that the object of much of this enterprise is to try to establish the theoretical utility and the nature of a specialised visuo-spatial system, then at least one of the prerequisites (i.e. a single cognitive resource underlying performance) cannot apply. Thus, equating levels of performance does not guarantee equivalent cognitive processing load. It simply shows that two different tasks can produce equivalent levels on two indicators of performance, given appropriate task demands.

On the evidence discussed so far, there remains considerable uncertainty as to whether performance of the Brooks visuo-spatial task really does rely primarily on a specialised visuo-spatial system or on general-purpose resources. It is also a moot point as to which aspects of functional cognition would be involved in initial encoding of the material, in maintaining the material during a retention interval, and in retrieving the material. Given the suggestion from Quinn's data that a general processing load may be crucial, it would be useful to provide a more direct test of just how much of a general load is involved in the Brooks tasks, given their pivotal role in the theoretical development of visuo-spatial working memory.

One attempt at such a direct test was carried out by Alice Salway (Logie & Salway, 1990; Salway, 1991) who was interested in using a technique known as random generation as a possible indicator of central executive functioning, or of allocation of attention (e.g. Baddeley, 1966c; Evans, 1978; Hayes & Broadbent, 1988; Wagenaar, 1972). Random generation involves asking subjects to generate at random items from a well known and well defined set such as the alphabet or the numbers one to ten. In the latter case subjects might produce a sequence such as "3-7-1-8-4-6-4-8-9-2 ... " and so on. A number of studies have shown that random generation appears to involve executive-like cognitive resources in that subjects have to keep track of the frequency with which they generate each item, and to inhibit well learned sequences such as "1-2-3-4-5" or items from outside the set for example "13". Random generation disrupts tasks normally associated with executive processing such as card sorting (Baddeley, 1966c).

Salway equated levels of control performance on the Brooks matrix and the Brooks verbal task, and then asked subjects to perform each version of the task concurrently with oral random generation of numbers at a one per second rate. She also looked at performance with concurrent articulatory suppression and with tapping four switches in a square pattern. Results in terms of the percentage correct on each of the Brooks tasks are shown in Fig. 4.4. What is clear from the figure is that articulatory suppression disrupted performance on the Brooks verbal task but not the Brooks spatial task, whereas tapping four switches had the converse effect. What is also clear is that random generation had a much larger disruptive effect on both Brooks tasks, and statistically, the effect was greater for the matrix task. That is, even though performance on the verbal and matrix tasks were equated before the experiment, verbal random generation disrupted an ostensibly visuo-spatial memory task more than it disrupted a verbal memory task. This raises the strong suspicion that the Brooks tasks place substantial demands on general-purpose resources, with the visuo-spatial version demanding the larger share of such resources.

Another way to approach the problems with interpreting interference effects on the Brooks tasks is to look at performance levels on the same

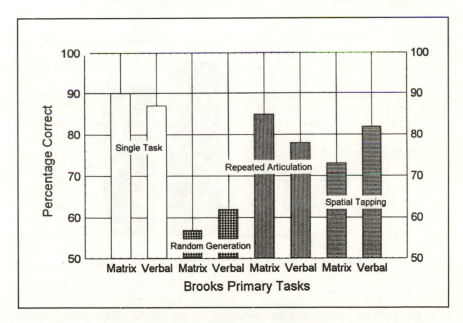

FIG. 4.4. Performance of the Brooks matrix and verbal tasks performed alone and concurrently with secondary tasks. Data from Salway (1991).

task rather than on different tasks. The dual-task methodology allows us to do just that. Instead of comparing performance on the two Brooks tasks, we can compare performance on a single secondary task that is combined in turn with recall of Brooks verbal material or of the number matrix pattern. In this sense we are turning the experiment around, treating the two Brooks tasks as secondary tasks, each of which is combined with a single primary task. With judicious choice of such a primary task where we are fairly confident of a general processing load we might be in a position to determine the relative general processing load involved in each of the Brooks tasks. In Salway's experiments this was accomplished by examining performance on the random generation task as a function of whichever Brooks task it accompanied. The data for this comparison are shown in Fig. 4.5 in the form of the Evans (1978) RNG index of redundancy, where a higher number indicates more redundancy in the responses, or less randomness (i.e. poorer performance). Here again, it appears that the Brooks matrix task resulted in the greatest impairment in performance, although the interaction shown in Fig. 4.5 just failed to reach significance, $F(1,46)=3.37$; $P=0.073$. Nevertheless Salway's results support the suggestion from Quinn's data that the Brooks matrix task probably relies heavily on general-purpose resources, at least during encoding, and thus

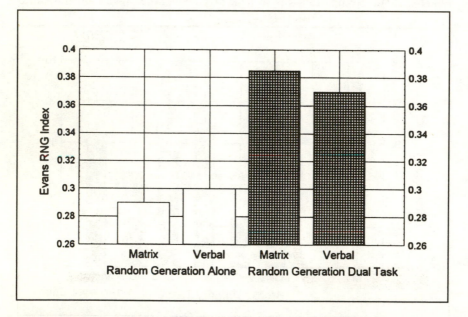

FIG. 4.5. Random generation performance (Evans, 1978, RNG Index) when performed alone and coupled with the Brooks matrix and verbal tasks. Data from Salway (1991).

cannot be taken as clear evidence for the use of a specialised visuo-spatial temporary memory system.

Working Memory and Complex Cognitive Skills

An opportunity to carry out a further investigation of the general load associated with the Brooks material arose from a project concerned with the role of working memory in learning and performing complex cognitive tasks. Logie et al. (1989) studied a small group of subjects learning to perform a complex computer game known as Space Fortress. A diagram of the screen layout for the game is shown in Fig. 4.6.[1]

Space Fortress involved a high level of perceptuo-motor control of a space ship which was manoeuvred around the screen (in a simulated frictionless environment) using a joystick. The game also involved accurate timing of responses, a verbal short-term memory load and the development of long-term and short-term strategies. The general aim of this work was to determine whether performance on the Space Fortress task might be fruitfully subdivided into a number of subcomponent skills. Our approach was to test this directly by means of the secondary task procedures that had proved fruitful in the development of working memory.

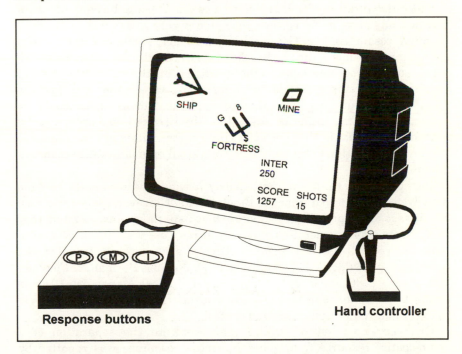

FIG. 4.6. Layout of display and controls for the Space Fortress game used by Logie et al. (1989).

We employed a wide range of secondary tasks chosen to examine the cognitive demands of 17 identifiable components of Space Fortress out of more than 50 measures of performance that were recorded. For the purposes of the discussion here I shall describe the findings for two of these tasks, namely the Brooks matrix and verbal tasks.

In the early stages of training, subjects' performance on Space Fortress was very severely impaired by concurrent performance of either of the Brooks tasks. There was no evidence of differential interference; just a massive, across-the-board performance impairment. In contrast, none of the other secondary tasks had such a general effect on performance. For example a secondary task involving mental comparisons between locations on an imaged map affected only specifically perceptuo-motor control on the game.

After the subjects were more highly practised on the game they began to show differential disruption, with different clusters of performance measures affected by the two different Brooks tasks. The verbal task tended to affect measures of short-term verbal memory load, whereas the matrix task tended to affect components of the game involving perceptuo-motor control.

The interpretation of these findings was that during the early stages of practice, adequate game performance placed very heavy demands on all cognitive resources, (e.g. Gopher, Weil, & Siegel, 1989), and the general processing demands of the two Brooks tasks were indeed fairly substantial. When subjects became more highly practised on the game, the general cognitive processing demands for performance were rather less, and the specific verbal or visuo-spatial nature of the Brooks tasks could be demonstrated. The upshot of this is that the Brooks tasks are generally quite difficult. That is, they both place heavy demands on general cognitive resources in addition to their demands on verbal or visuo-spatial cognitive resources.

In the light of these findings, clearly it would be unwise to rely too heavily on data derived from the Brooks tasks. However, there remains a strong case for a specialised temporary visuo-spatial memory system that is separate from general-purpose resources, because in most of the published reports discussed so far the Brooks tasks were not the only tasks used (see e.g. Baddeley & Lieberman, 1980; Farmer, Berman, & Fletcher, 1986; Logie, 1986; Logie et al., 1989; Logie et al, 1990; Morris, 1987). From among these same studies there is also evidence that this system has a role to play in movement planning and control.

One very neat set of studies that speak to the separation of a visuo-spatial resource from general-purpose resources was reported by Farmer et al. (1986). These authors took the suggestion from Phillips and Christie (1977a;b) that if there is a separate visuo-spatial system then it should be possible to find tasks that place heavy demands on the specialised system without a requirement for central executive capacity. Such a task would interfere with visuo-spatial processing and storage, but would not interfere with the performance of tasks that have a low visuo-spatial load but place substantial demands on general-purpose resources.

Farmer and his colleagues devised a visual tracking task that involved tapping four metal plates placed in a square arrangement on a table in front of the subject. On the basis of previous studies of tracking, this task was taken as one that loaded specialised visuo-spatial resources without loading the central executive. They also used a complementary task, articulatory suppression, to investigate the role of the specialised verbal system, the phonological loop.

As their first primary task, Farmer et al. adopted the Baddeley (1968) AB reasoning task described in Chapter 1. This was thought to place heavy demands on the central executive because of its reliance on logical reasoning but to have a minimal visuo-spatial component. It also appeared to have very little reliance on verbal short-term storage. You may recall that Baddeley and Hitch (1974) found that subjects could hold a sequence of three digits and perform the AB reasoning task without mutual interference. Moreover, Hitch and Baddeley (1976) reported that articulatory suppression had only a very small effect on performance of this task.

Farmer et al. (1986) found that concurrent spatial tapping had no effect whatsoever on performance of even the most demanding of the AB reasoning problems. Articulatory suppression had a small disruptive effect but only for the most difficult problems.

It is possible that these results arose because neither articulatory suppression nor the tapping task was particularly difficult. Thus it is possible that even with the most difficult AB reasoning problems there was still residual capacity in the central executive to perform the tapping test efficiently. In order to test this Farmer et al. replaced the AB reasoning test with a spatial reasoning task which would be more likely to rely on visuo-spatial processing. This was the Manikin test (Benson & Gedye, 1963) which involved the display of a manikin figure holding in one hand a circle, and in the other hand a square. One of these shapes was displayed as a target below the figure. The subject's task was to indicate in which hand the target shape was being held. Examples of the kind of stimuli are shown in Fig. 4.7 where the targets are shown as black or white circles. The manikin figure could be in a number of orientations: facing away from or towards the subject, and upright or inverted. In this case there was no effect of articulatory suppression but a substantial impairment was observed with the tapping task.

An initial conclusion from these experiments is that they support the relatively uncontroversial dissociation between verbal and visuo-spatial

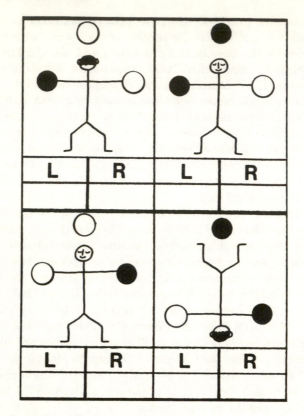

FIG. 4.7. Example stimuli for the Manikin test.

processing. What is rather more surprising about these results is that the AB reasoning task appears to rely on resources other than the phonological loop or visuo-spatial processing. This may give some insight into the characteristics of a central executive involved in reasoning, but this is not a topic for debate in this volume. More pertinent here is that the results also support a distinction between the possibly general-purpose executive system (responsible for reasoning) and visuo-spatial processing involved in tapping and in the Manikin test.

Encoding versus Maintenance

There remains another puzzle arising from Quinn's work, namely the finding that concurrent movement had a disruptive effect during encoding of the Brooks spatial material but not if the secondary task was performed during a retention interval. It seemed as if encoding involved a cognitive system that also played a role in movement, but that the storage function was provided by a system that was quite independent of initial encoding.

In the case of the Farmer et al. studies the tapping task was performed concurrently with encoding of both the AB reasoning task and the Manikin test so their data cannot address this particular difficulty. Indeed much of the work on visuo-spatial temporary memory discussed so far has been concerned with visuo-spatial storage and processing as studied during encoding and recall of visual and spatial information. There is very little literature addressing the means by which information is *retained* in visuo-spatial memory tasks.

One further series of studies (in addition to those of Quinn) did directly compare interference effects at encoding with those during a retention interval. Morris (1987) presented subjects with circles shown in random positions on an otherwise blank screen. After the circles were removed subjects had to draw the circles in their appropriate positions. Accurate recall of the positions of the circles was disrupted by non-visual tracking performed concurrently with the presentation of the circle display. However, there was no disruption associated with tracking performed only during a retention interval between offset of the circles and the start of recall of circle positions. Articulatory suppression had no disruptive effect whether performed at encoding or during the retention interval.

Taking the Morris and Quinn results together they seem to suggest that whatever system is involved in encoding the Brooks matrix patterns or the circle patterns is also involved in controlling movement. In terms of the working memory model such findings present something of an anomaly because it seems reasonable to assume that a visuo-spatial scratch pad ought to be involved in temporary *retention* of visual and spatial information as well as its encoding.

A possible interpretation is that the *encoding* of such material places a load on general attentional resources. If we assume that movement control also requires general attentional resources then the disruption observed in both the Quinn and the Morris studies can be interpreted as a general distraction effect rather than reflecting competition for specialised visuo-spatial resources. I have already argued about the inherent difficulty of the Brooks tasks and the argument could in principle also apply to the Morris tasks.

The Role of Spatial Resources

What then is the role of visuo-spatial working memory in these tasks? One possibility is that it is involved in retention rather than encoding and that encoding is more the prerogative of the central executive. There certainly is evidence that the central executive is involved in learning, of which encoding is an important part (see e.g. Baddeley, Lewis, Eldridge, & Thomson, 1984).

One way to approach this apparent setback for visuo-spatial working memory is to consider in more detail the tasks used both by Morris and by Quinn. Their results cause a problem only if we assume that the cognitive processes involved in retaining the Brooks matrix or the Morris circles are similar to the cognitive processes involved in encoding that same material.

In the Brooks matrix task for example subjects are instructed to imagine moving through the squares of an imaged square matrix. Once encoding is complete, however, the subject need retain only a static pattern of the appropriate squares in the imaged matrix. They do not have to retain a sequence of imagined movements. This imagined static pattern can then be used as a mnemonic for later recall.

Thus we can envisage an essentially spatial process of imagined movement during encoding, but something rather more like a static visual image being used during retention. The recall process may also be spatial if we assume that subjects mentally scan their visual image in order to report the retained pattern. Thus a *spatial* process may be involved during encoding and retrieval of a sequence of verbal instructions that describe spatial positions. A *visual* temporary memory system could be responsible for retaining the imaged pattern of numbers in specific locations in a matrix. The same argument could apply to encoding and retention of a display of circles on a screen as in Morris's (1987) experiments.

This seems an appropriate point at which to return to the issue of whether the visuo-spatial scratch pad comprises one or two mechanisms. Many of the data described earlier could readily be accounted for if we were to assume two mechanisms, one spatial (in the sense of the loose definition given previously) and the other visual. It is clear that the initial process of encoding may not only be spatial but also effortful. That is, encoding uses general-purpose resources instead of or in addition to specialised spatial processing, at least in the case of the Brooks material and the Morris circles. Thus the visual temporary memory system would perhaps be more like a subsidiary system that requires little in the way of central executive or general-purpose resources to provide a temporary storage function.

However, there are still some questions unanswered. For example, need we necessarily tie in the spatial memory system with an effortful encoding process? I have already discussed evidence which suggests that the Brooks tasks are inherently effortful, and there remains the possibility of a distinction between memory for genuinely spatial material and the processes involved in initial encoding and in retrieval. That is, how do subjects retain sequences of movement? Do they continue to rely on general-purpose resources or can they rely on a non-executive memory system for movement? Given the results reported by Farmer et al. (1986) it seems that there is indeed such a separate spatial system.

Some further evidence for this last interpretation comes from a study by myself and a colleague, Clelia Marchetti (Logie & Marchetti, 1991). In this experiment subjects were required to retain information from one or other of two kinds of visually presented displays which we labelled respectively visual or spatial. The visual display comprised the simultaneous presentation of squares, each in a different hue of the same colour, and each shown in a different position on a computer screen. Thus, for example, the squares on any one trial could be shown all in different shades of red or all in different shades of blue. This procedure was adopted to encourage subjects to use a visual code for the colours rather than to rely on colour names. The spatial display consisted of a series of squares (each in a different shade of the same colour) presented one after another, and each at different locations on the screen.

After either the visual display or the spatial display there followed a retention interval of 10 seconds between presentation and a subsequent recognition test. In the case of the visual display subjects were shown squares in the same locations as before, but on 50% of occasions one of the colour hues had been changed. In the case of the spatial display the sequence of squares was repeated with the squares shown in the same locations as before, but on 50% of trials the order of presentation of the squares was altered.

Thus in the visual condition, subjects had to remember the shade of the colour presented in a particular location on the screen. In the spatial condition, subjects had to retain the order in which the squares had appeared at particular locations on the screen.

A primary motivation for this experiment was to explore the characteristics of the memory functions used to store spatial and/or visual material. Therefore we added two conditions involving contrasting second-ary tasks performed during the 10-second retention interval. In one condi-tion, the retention interval was filled by a concurrent movement task, along the lines of that used by Quinn (1988; 1991) where subjects had to make unseen arm movements. The contrasting secondary task involved present-ing irrelevant pictures. You may recall the evidence that this latter kind of material interferes with the use of a visual imagery mnemonic (Logie, 1986) and the retention of other kinds of visual material (Matthews, 1983).

If the disruptive effects reported by Quinn (1988; 1991) and by Morris (1987) were primarily due to general distraction during stimulus encoding, then we would anticipate no disruptive effect of either secondary task during the retention interval. However, if separate systems are involved in retaining respectively spatial and visual material, then we would expect that the movement task would disrupt memory for a presented sequence of spatial locations, while the irrelevant pictures (Logie, 1986; Matthews, 1983) should disrupt retention of the colour hues.

The results are shown in Fig. 4.8 from which it was clear that the differential disruption appeared, as predicted by the distinction between specialised systems for retaining respectively visual and spatial information.

This finding was replicated by Tresch, Sinnamon, and Seamon (1993) who asked subjects either to remember the location of a single dot on a screen, or to remember the form of a presented geometric shape. During a 10-second retention interval subjects were either given a movement discrimination task or a colour discrimination task, followed by a recognition memory test for either dot location or for the presented geometric form. As Marchetti and I found, the interpolated movement task disrupted retention of dot location but did not disrupt memory for the form, whereas the colour discrimination task disrupted retention of the geometric form but did not affect memory for dot location.

These results are consistent with separate visual and spatial temporary memory systems; however the picture is still not entirely clear. For example, how is maintenance in such systems accomplished? In a paper published in 1989 (Logie, 1989) I suggested that visuo-spatial short-term memory might comprise two functions; a passive visual store and an active

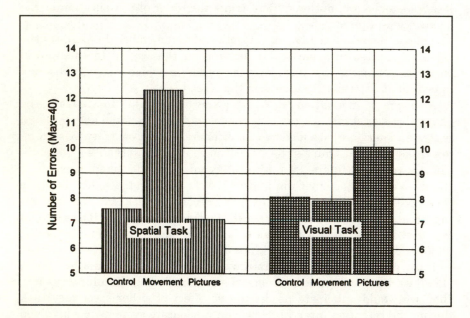

FIG. 4.8. Data from Logie and Marchetti (1991).

rehearsal process, with the latter function related to the control of movement. The rehearsal process would also be akin to some form of mental scanning of the visual representation. Watkins, Peynircioglu, and Brems (1984) have provided evidence for a pictorial rehearsal function, and a number of the studies that I discussed earlier have provided independent support for the relationship between visual imagery and the retention of movements.

According to this interpretation, the retention of the colour hues in the Logie and Marchetti experiment was primarily the responsibility of a passive visual store. Irrelevant visual input is thought to have obligatory access to this store, thus causing disruption of its contents during a retention interval. Retention of a series of movements would be accomplished by the rehearsal mechanism. Because the rehearsal mechanism is also involved in the control of movement, a requirement to generate a series of irrelevant movements would disrupt this rehearsal mechanism, leading to poorer recall of the original movement sequence.

This interpretation has some considerable explanatory power, and has a highly seductive symmetry with the phonological loop described earlier. In this respect the model of the phonological loop as a framework for the VSSP has proved to be fruitful, although I would urge some caution in taking the analogy too far. Also, it generates a number of questions as to the role of the rehearsal function in retaining complex static visual images, as well as retaining information about movement to targets (e.g. Smyth & Pendleton, 1989). In so doing, it provides an extremely useful heuristic for the exploration of the relationships between movement control, visual short-term memory, and the human capacity to generate and manipulate visual images. The model is presented here only in outline, and it will be discussed in more detail in Chapter six. However prior to that it would be useful to discuss the neuropsychological evidence pertaining to visual and spatial temporary memory, to complement the data from healthy subjects that I have discussed so far.

NOTES

1.   I am grateful to Peter Bates of the Psychology Department, University of Aberdeen for drawing this figure.

CHAPTER FIVE

Neuropsychology

Although there is a very large literature on the neuropsychology of memory, and a well established literature on verbal short-term memory deficits, the existing neuropsychological literature is relatively light in its discussion of impairments of visuo-spatial working memory. There is certainly an established body of work on visuo-spatial deficits, some of which has explored deficits of imagery (e.g. Farah, 1984). Given my earlier discussion of the link between visual imagery and visuo-spatial working memory, a discussion of patients with imagery deficits as well as with other forms of visuo-spatial deficit should be informative. In this chapter I shall first discuss neuropsychological evidence for the dissociation between verbal and visuo-spatial working memory. This will be followed by a discussion of patients with varying forms of visuo-spatial deficits, and in particular visual imagery deficits. The chapter will conclude with a discussion of the neuropsychological case for a distinction between visual and spatial short-term memory as mooted in Chapter 4.

DISSOCIATIONS AND DEFICITS

There are a number of documented patients with reported visuo-spatial short-term memory deficits in the absence of equivalent deficits for verbal material. For example, De Renzi and Nichelli (1975) described two cases of patients with damage to the right hemisphere who had scores of 2.5 on the Corsi block span task. This is a performance level in the pathological range. These same patients achieved scores of around 7 on digit span. They also had normal performance on tests of long-term visuo-spatial memory. In that same study De Renzi and Nichelli reported that among a group of 32 patients with right hemisphere damage (including the two patients just described), performance on Corsi span was notably poor in relation to their performance on digit span tasks. A contrasting group of 39 patients with left hemisphere damage showed the opposite pattern. De Renzi, Faglioni, and Previdi (1977) replicated the observed link between right hemisphere damage and Corsi span impairment in a further group of patients with right hemisphere damage.

More recently, Hanley, Young, and Pearson (1991) reported a single case, E.L.D., with right hemisphere damage who showed very poor performance on Corsi blocks, on the Brooks (1967) matrix task, on mental rotation, and in using visual imagery mnemonics. This same patient was unimpaired in her ability to recall letter sequences with auditory and with visual presentation. She also showed evidence of word length and phonological similarity effects.

In studies of visual rather than visuo-spatial short-term memory deficits, there is evidence for an involvement of the left hemisphere rather than the right. In a group study, Warrington and Rabin (1971) reported visual short-term memory deficits that were most evident in those of their patients who had damage to the posterior region of the left hemisphere. Performance was measured on a "visual span of apprehension" test. For this task, the patients were shown a sequence of letters, digits, or lines and curves for brief periods ranging from 50msec to 160msec, and were required to report as many of the presented items as possible. The left posterior damaged patients were impaired in their ability to report random strings of digits or letters, or of lines and curves. These patients were relatively unimpaired in reporting letter strings that were approximations to words. They also appeared to have auditory digit spans in the normal range. Patients with right hemisphere lesions showed no deficits in span of apprehension when compared with non brain-damaged control subjects.

In a study of two single cases, Ross (1980) reported what he termed loss of "recent visual memory" in patients with damage to the right occipital lobe. One of the patients also had damage in the left occipital lobe. These patients could copy drawings and could reproduce patterns if they were asked to draw them immediately after they had been removed. However they were unable to remember anything of visually presented patterns if there was a brief delay between removal of the pattern and the request to draw, or to recognise the pattern. At least one of the patients made extensive use of verbal codes to supplement his poor temporary visual memory. For example, if shown a pen for a few seconds, after a three-minute delay, he could correctly identify a pen from distractor objects such as a comb, a pencil, or some chalk. However he was not retaining information about the visual appearance of the pen because a few moments later he was unable to select the presented pen from among several other pens serving as distractors. He was also unable to recall the layout of objects in a room after a brief presentation, and after a delay of one minute during which his eyes were closed. Verbal short-term memory and long-term visual memory were unimpaired in both patients. For example, one of the patients could accurately recall and draw the layout of his parents' house.

Beyn and Knyazeva (1962) reported a single case of a patient with bilateral damage to the occipital lobe who was able to copy drawings of objects but was unable to continue copying after the original drawings had been removed. He also had considerable difficulty drawing objects from long-term memory.

There are in addition a number of patients who show the converse pattern. For example, patient K.F., mentioned in Chapter 1 (Shallice & Warrington, 1970; Warrington & Shallice, 1972) could recall a sequence of just two digits which he had heard. In contrast K.F. could recall a sequence of four visually presented digits. When he made errors with visually presented letters, these errors tended to be based on visual confusions rather than acoustic confusions. As I mentioned earlier, most normal subjects tend to produce acoustic confusions with visually presented, verbal material. This suggests that normal subjects usually translate the visually presented words, letters, or digits into a phonologically based code for retention in a phonologically based store. It appeared, then, that K.F. attempted to retain information using relatively intact visual short-term storage functions while his phonologically based, verbal short-term storage system was severely impaired. In contrast, normal subjects typically can retain more auditorily presented items than visually presented items (e.g. Conrad, 1964). Similar patterns have been reported for other patients with verbal short-term memory deficits (e.g. Basso et al., 1982; Saffran & Marin, 1975). In particular, patient P.V., to whom I referred earlier in the book, has been extensively studied as a relatively pure case of someone with a deficit in the phonological loop component of working memory (e.g. Basso et al., 1982; Vallar & Baddeley, 1984). Basso et al. reported P.V.'s performance on visual and auditory versions of the Brown-Peterson task where recall of verbal material is required after a filled delay. With one consonant for recall, after a three-second filled delay, P.V. achieved perfect recall performance with visual presentation, but recalled correctly on only half of the trials for auditory presentation.

One approach to interpreting patterns of sparing and impairment in neuropsychological patients is to suggest that impairments might be shown by tasks that are more difficult. That is, a damaged brain may have more difficulty with cognitively demanding tasks. It is clear from the patients discussed here that this cannot be the case, in view of the double dissociations observed between patients.

Impairments of both spatial and visual temporary memory have also been demonstrated in patients with dementia of the Alzheimer type and in patients with Parkinson's disease. Baddeley, Della Sala, and Spinnler (1991) observed that one of their Alzheimer patients showed a pathological score on tests of visual short-term memory, but had verbal short-term memory performance within the normal range. One of their other patients showed exactly the converse pattern, demonstrating a double dissociation. In a study of 18 Alzheimer's disease patients, Perani and colleagues (1993) observed that five of their patients were below the pathological cut-off score on Corsi block span, while two of the patients were impaired on digit span. However in most studies of Alzheimer's patients, verbal short-term memory tends to be impaired more frequently than is visuo-spatial short-term memory (Cantone, Orsini, Grossi, & De Michele, 1978; Morris & Baddeley, 1988). In some studies, both visuo-spatial and verbal short-term and long-term memory deficits have been found in Alzheimer's patients (Spinnler, Della Sala, Bandera, & Baddeley, 1988; Sullivan & Sagar, 1991). In the Sullivan and Sagar (1991) report, they noted that a group of Parkinson's patients were impaired on visuo-spatial short-term memory while long-term visuo-spatial memory was intact. In their group of Alzheimer's patients, both long- and short-term visuo-spatial memory were impaired.

Further evidence for a distinction between visuo-spatial and verbal short-term memory comes from studies of brain activity in normal subjects either by means of scanning techniques such as positron emission tomography (PET) which measures brain metabolism, or monitoring brain electrical activity such as via event-related brain potentials (ERP). Ruchkin et al. (1992) recorded ERPs from a group of young healthy subjects while they were asked to retain visuo-spatial material in the form of random two-dimensional displays, or to retain phonologically based material in the form of pronounceable non-words. The ERP patterns were quite different for the two different kinds of material. Indeed, Ruchkin et al. reported that these two distinct ERP patterns also differed from a third observed pattern which appeared to be associated with central executive functioning. Their results are supported by previous work showing, in separate studies, differential ERPs for phonological memory tasks (Rugg, 1984) and for tasks involving memory for visual features of faces (Barrett, Rugg, & Perrett, 1988).

Perani et al. (1993) carried out PET scans on 18 patients with Alzheimer's disease, and reported that scores on spatial short-term memory were best predicted by the scan-derived metabolic values from the right parietal and frontal associative areas. Verbal short-term memory was more closely associated with the temporal, parietal, and frontal areas of the left hemisphere.

IMAGERY AND IMAGERY DEFICITS

Some hints about the role of various brain structures in imagery tasks have arisen from a wide range of studies of patients with imagery deficits, and from a few studies of brain activity during imagery tasks performed by normal adult volunteers. Examples of the latter were carried out by Goldenberg and colleagues (e.g. Goldenberg et al., 1991). They have used SPECT (single photon emission computer tomography) to study the differential patterns of blood flow in the brain during visual imagery tasks and during acoustic imagery tasks. The blood flow patterns were quite distinct in the two tasks. In particular the acoustic imagery tasks were associated with increased blood flow in both hippocampal regions and in the right temporal lobe, whereas both imagery tasks resulted in an increase in blood flow in the left inferior occipital region and the left thalamus. However on questioning the subjects Goldenberg et al. found that subjects reported using visual imagery for both the visual and the acoustic imagery tasks. They concluded that visual imagery was most likely associated with activity in the left hemisphere, in the occipital lobe, and in the thalamus.

Turning to imagery deficits, Farah (1984) has reported some very convincing evidence drawn from a re-examination of previously published single cases, each of whom appeared to have deficits of visual imagery. In her review she notes that different aspects of imagery ability are impaired in different patients. The patterns of impairment map well onto Kosslyn's model of imagery referred to in Chapter 2. For example, eight of the cases she described appeared to have an image generation deficit. That is they could perceive objects, describe and recognise objects, and draw objects that were present. Despite this they could not describe objects from long-term memory, or draw objects from long-term memory, and denied having visual imagery. All of these subjects appeared to have lesions in the left parieto-occipital area of the brain, and they seemed to have an image generation deficit in the absence of any evidence of visual agnosia. That is, they must have had access to information in their long-term memories about the link between the appearance of objects and the object name, in order for them to be able to identify those objects correctly. However they seemed unable to conjure up mental images of the objects. This points to a dissociation between the system responsible for retrieving information from long-term memory and for creating an image, and the processes involved in object recognition.

A further 13 patients in Farah's review could describe objects, draw objects that were present, and detect whether objects were visually presented. However they could not recognise or identify objects, nor could they describe or draw objects when presented with the object name. Farah argued that this demonstrated an impairment in access to long-term visual representations of objects to allow identification, but left the patients with a means to process the physical features of presented objects in order to draw them. Presumably the process of drawing would require some form of temporary visual storage, in order to store the appearance of the part of the object while they looked at and produced the drawing (van Sommers, 1989). Even if the subjects frequently looked back at the object, there is still a requirement for temporary visual storage.

Farah's report is extremely useful in pointing out how previously published reports of neuropsychological patients can be used to inform contemporary theories of cognition. The disadvantage of course is that it is not possible to go back and re-test these patients. Nor can a great deal be gleaned about the neuroanatomical correlates of the impairments, because although the pattern of functional deficit was relatively homogeneous across these patients, there was no clear common anatomical locus for their lesions. Moreover, the initial investigations of these patients were not motivated by the model of visual imagery favoured by Farah, and by Kosslyn and colleagues, and the data are necessarily being interpreted *post hoc* (Sergent, 1989). This has the implication that a number of key questions cannot be asked. For example an inability to draw an object in response to the name coupled with a failure to identify an object could indicate a severing of the links between the name of the object and its visual form. That is, the patients might still have access to the long-term memory representation of the visual form of the object when presented with the object, but be unable to access that form via the name. This leads to the question as to whether the patients knew how to use the presented object as well as to draw it. That is, could they access object semantics, even if they were unable to name the object? Another important issue is whether the patients from either group could draw a picture of an object that had been presented for a short time and which was then removed from view. In other words, could these patients draw objects from visual short-term memory, without the opportunity to refresh the contents of that memory system by repeatedly looking back at the object?

This last question was addressed at least in part in a single case study reported by Riddoch (1990). Case D.W. suffered damage to the left temporo-parietal region as a result of a cerebro-vascular bleed. The patient was unable to draw objects from long-term memory, or to perform mental rotation when tested with letter forms or with the Manikin test (Benson & Gedye, 1963; Farmer et al., 1986; Ratcliff, 1979). However he showed unimpaired performance in object identification, and he could copy a picture that was physically present. In addition, the patient had little difficulty drawing a set of letter forms immediately after they had been removed from view. Performance was very similar when he was required to wait for a period of 10 seconds before drawing the stimuli. In other words, the patient appeared to have a difficulty generating images from long-term memory, but had access to long-term memory that allowed for normal object recognition. More important, he could retain visually presented information for at least 10 seconds after the stimulus had been removed. Riddoch interprets her data as suggesting that the system for generating and manipulating visual images might well be distinct from that involved in short-term visual storage.

Further support for this view comes from an informal study reported by Frick (1987) who described two subjects with an apparent deficit in generating conscious visual images. The same individuals performed normally on tests of visual short-term memory. Frick's subjects were selected largely on self report and with no reported evidence of brain damage, and the data were somewhat informal. However together with data like those from Riddoch, there is a nagging doubt as to whether conscious visual imagery and visual short-term memory are as closely related as has been assumed. Within the rubric of working memory, one speculative suggestion is that conscious visual imagery may be more closely linked to central executive function than to a visuo-spatial temporary storage function. In this light of this, it would be interesting to test the central executive functioning of subjects with imagery deficits. This would allow a systematic exploration as to whether there is a segment of the architecture of working memory devoted to visual imagery, or whether imagery relies on a general purpose, flexible system. I shall explore this suggestion in more detail in Chapter 6 when discussing related data from normal adult subjects.

VISUAL NEGLECT

Among the disorders of visuo-spatial cognition, one of the most intriguing involves apparent loss of information from one half of visual space, normally on the left, and normally associated with right hemisphere damage. This disorder, which occurs in the absence of peripheral visual acuity problems, has generated a great deal of debate in that it touches on the nature of the visual representation of the world and of conscious experience (e.g. Bisiach, 1993). It has been interpreted both as a deficit of attention and as a deficit of representation. Although the disorder was first reported in 1876 by Hughlings Jackson, it was only in the mid 1970s that patients with this disorder appeared to any great extent in the research literature.

One of the classic reports of this disorder was by Bisiach and Luzzatti (1978) who asked two Milanese neglect patients to imagine themselves standing in the Cathedral Square in Milan (Piazza del Duomo). When they imagined themselves facing the cathedral from the far end of the square, they accurately described the buildings on their "imagined" right. However they failed to mention buildings on the left side of the square. When asked to imagine facing in the opposite direction, standing on the cathedral steps with the cathedral building behind them, they described buildings on the other side of the square that they had previously failed to mention, but omitted descriptions of buildings that would have been to their left, and which they had successfully reported a few moments before. One of the patients was also asked to describe his studio, imagining himself sitting at his desk, or facing his desk. The studio was a room in which the patient had spent a great deal of time, and with which he was highly familiar. As before, he tended to describe items on the right of the studio, but omitted items that were on the left. Both for the Piazza del Duomo and for the studio, the patients omitted even very large and salient items on their imagined left such as the Royal Palace in the Square, and an upright piano in the studio.

An interesting aspect of the observations is that despite their disorder, both patients did report a small number of features on the neglected side after some delay or with some prompting from the experimenter. This might suggest that they have some residual information available on the neglected side, and that their disorder represents a bias rather than complete loss of access to the information. However it is also worth noting that the patients were very familiar with the Piazza del Duomo, and the second patient had used his studio for many years. The patients were not amnesic and there is no reason why they could not use verbal codes to help them recall either (a) their reports from the alternative imaginary perspective on the previous test session the day before, or (b) from verbally encoded information about the target environment. For example Bisiach and Luzzatti's second patient initially failed to mention a piano which was on his neglected side when sitting at the desk. He did however report the piano after some hesitation and after he had mentioned most of the objects on the other side of the room. Bisiach and Luzzatti noted that this patient had spent a great deal of time playing the piano in his lifetime, and that verbal knowledge of a highly familiar environment would be sufficient to allow a report of information from the neglected side. For example from my verbal knowledge of my own office, I can report that I have a desk, two bookcases, a round table, two filing cabinets, and a computer, without having to construct a visual image of the contents of my office or to consult a mental representation of their layout. It is also clear from other studies of neglect patients that when they are asked to draw a clock, some patients are perfectly aware that the numbers should run from 1 to 12. Even although their drawing depicts only the right side of the clock, it is not uncommon (although this does not occur in every case) for numbers from the left side of the clock to appear squeezed into the right side shown in the drawing. One other possibility in the case of the Bisiach and Luzzatti patients is of course that the subjects attempted to alter their imagined orientation spontaneously, without instructions from the experimenter. That is, the delay in responding could have been sufficient for the subjects to imagine themselves walking back to the other end of the Cathedral square, and turning around!

Whether there is no information or just partial information available on the neglected side, it is clear that these patients have a severe asymmetric impairment, and since the seminal studies in the 1970s there is now a large literature on the topic with a range of associated and relatively well established findings. For example, when asked to draw everyday objects either from memory or when physically present, neglect patients tend to produce drawings of just one side of the object. When asked to cross out all the occurrences of a single letter on a sheet of randomly arranged letters, they tend to cross out only those letters on the right side. Similarly when asked to indicate the mid point of a line, their indication tends to be grossly skewed to the right. Many neglect patients also tend to ignore the left side of their body, and some deny that their left arm is actually part of their body. There are also cases of patients with neglect of the right side, but such patients are relatively rare. A recent excellent review of this area is given in Bisiach (1993).

The nature of the deficit could be thought of in at least two ways. One view is that the visual scene is adequately encoded, but that patients tend to ignore half of the encoded representation, with a substantial attentional bias towards the right (e.g. Kinsbourne, 1977, 1993; Riddoch & Humphreys, 1983). With a slightly different emphasis Posner, Cohen, and Rafal (1982) suggest that there is an attentional bias away from the left rather than specifically towards the right. In contrast, Bisiach among others has suggested that the deficit lies in the representation (see also Caramazza & Hillis, 1990), with information essentially omitted from the neglected side. He has pointed out that the attentional hypothesis runs the risk of requiring an homunculus which examines the visual representation displayed on some form of internal screen. This leads to questions about the nature of the homunculus and the possibility of an infinite regress. In support of the representational view, Bisiach, Luzzatti, and Perani (1979) asked their patients to look at a series of abstract cloud-like patterns, and to decide whether pairs of patterns differed or not. However the patterns could only be seen one part at a time while they were moved behind a narrow slit. Thus judgements could be made only if the subjects were able to construct an accurate visual representation of the patterns derived from a small amount of changing information in central vision. The neglect patients failed to discriminate the items that differed only on the left side, despite the fact that all of the relevant information had been presented centrally. This experiment supports the notion that the phenomenon of neglect is based on the nature of the mental representation, although it does not rule out the possibility that the impairment is in attention to parts of the mental representation or due to an incomplete representation.

The debate is taken forward by Halligan and Marshall (1991) who demonstrated that neglect patients have available information that appears to affect their responses even if they fail to report information present in the left visual field. For example, Halligan and Marshall showed neglect patients pictures of houses, and in one of the pictures the left half of the house was depicted in flames. The patients denied noticing anything unusual about the houses, and reported that the two pictures looked the same, but when asked about which house they would prefer to live in they rejected the picture showing half of the house on fire. This points strongly to an attentional interpretation, in that the information appears to be represented in some form, but is largely ignored by the patient.

Further evidence for this kind of implicit processing of information in the neglected field comes from a study by McGlinchey-Berroth and colleagues (1993). Their patients were given a lexical decision task, with the words or non-words presented centrally. Prior to the presentation of each letter string, pictures appeared in either the left or the right visual field. Lexical decision times for real words were faster when the picture matched the subsequently presented word, and this occurred even when the picture primes were presented in the neglected hemifield.

What is notable here is that the data on priming effects and implicit processing cause difficulty for the representational view of neglect only if it is assumed that these effects arise from information contained in a coherent visual representation. If instead we assume that priming involves the temporary activation of long-term memory representations in the lexicon or semantic memory system, the data are still consistent with an "incomplete representation" view of neglect. Thus the impairment could lie in the mechanism that constructs the conscious visual representation from activated long-term memory traces. For example, we know already that neglect patients fail to construct a representation of the neglected side of objects whose features are drawn from long-term memory. A similar argument can be made about the Halligan and Marshall experiments on implicit processing. Presentation of a picture of a house on fire could activate long-term semantic memory networks comprising links between houses and fires and unpleasant consequences, without this information being incorporated in a conscious mental representation of the complete picture. Thus the stimulus information is reaching semantic memory, but the damaged neural functioning is preventing that information from reaching a conscious mental representation.

There is a continuing debate on this topic in the literature on cognitive neuropsychology. The attentional/representational issue remains as a focus of this debate. An additional issue concerns the representation of the relationship between egocentric and exocentric space. That is, does the cognitive system that is damaged in neglect patients hold information about the relationship between body parts and objects in the visual scene? Alternatively, does the disorder primarily affect the representation of the mutual relationships among objects in the world irrespective of the position of the body parts of the viewer? Bisiach has assumed the former (e.g. Bisiach, 1993), and moreover has stated explicitly that these spatial relationships are held in working memory. He does not give details as to the nature of the working memory system that he envisages might host this representation, but does refer explicitly to a visuo-spatial scratch pad referred to in the Baddeley and Lieberman (1980) paper. You may recall from Chapter 4 that Baddeley and Lieberman viewed the scratch pad as being primarily spatial rather than visual in nature. Bisiach suggests that visual neglect might be characterised as damage to that part of the visuo-spatial scratch pad that represents the left half of the spatial array. Presumably this would apply to a representation of the currently presented scene as well as for visuo-spatial representations generated from long-term memory.

In a more recent paper Halligan and Marshall (1992) argued strongly that it is highly misleading to think of visual neglect as a single form of disorder. They report for example that there are double dissociations among neglect patients, some of whom show an impairment in letter cancellation tasks but are unimpaired on line bisection tasks, whereas other patients show the converse. They conclude that there are likely to be a range of neglect disorders, each of which requires a cognitive explanation, and each of which would have its own set of neuropathological correlates. This raises complications for clinical approaches to hemi-neglect, for example in diagnosis and in development of possible neuropsychological rehabilitation. It also causes difficulties when developing general theories or explanations of hemi-neglect.

One way to tackle the problem of having different types of neglect patient would be to develop theories for each of the different forms of neglect. But this can be a perilous approach, potentially leading to the development of a different variant of the theory for each variant of the neuropsychological disorder. This gives the theories less generality and makes them less useful as a consequence. An alternative is to use the data derived from the neuropsychological patients to help develop general models of normal cognition. Thus we can attempt to develop a model of normal visuo-spatial cognition derived in part from studies of hemi-neglect patients, and in part from studies of normal subjects and from other groups of neuropsychological patients. We should then be able to use such a model to provide putative explanations for at least some of the various forms of hemi-neglect.

Assuming this is a primary objective, then what can these data tell us about the nature of normal visuo-spatial working memory? One conclusion that is fairly well supported by these data is that there is indeed a distinction between the visuo-spatial information that subjects potentially have available, and the information they are able to report explicitly. Another way of looking at this would be to say that there is a distinction between conscious experience of visuo-spatial information, possibly in the form of visuo-spatial imagery, and some semi-independent visuo-spatial temporary memory. Moreover, I have already suggested that the data on priming effects in neglect patients indicates that visuo-spatial information presented to the neglected field has access to semantic information in long-term memory. This information does not appear to be part of the representation in working memory. One tentative interpretation would be to suggest that priming results in temporary activation of long-term memory representations and this activation is sufficient to make information detectable only in tests of implicit processing. In normal subjects, the activation makes the information available for construction of a mental representation in working memory. However some forms of brain damage prevent this information from being included in that mental representation. Such a model has a number of additional implications. In particular it suggests that the contents of working memory might result from activation of long-term memory traces, and this is in contrast to the view of working memory as some form of gateway between stimulus input and long-term memory. Far from being a gateway, the contents of working memory are available only *after* that information has been processed in long-term memory. This view is consistent with the argument outlined towards the end of Chapter 1, and referred to elsewhere in the book. I shall explore the model further in Chapter 6 (see Fig. 6.6, p.127) when giving more detailed treatment to theory development in the area of visuo-spatial short-term memory. In the meantime, I would like to return to another major theme of this book, namely the hypothesised distinction between visual and spatial working memory, with respect to relevant evidence from studies of neuropsychological patients.

VISUAL OR SPATIAL DEFICITS?

The possibility of a spatial versus visual distinction discussed in Chapter 4 echoes a similar distinction current in the neuropsychological literature on the nature of the cognitive mechanisms involved in visual imagery.

I touched on neuropsychological evidence for the distinction earlier in this chapter. Dissociations among cognitive functions are convincing when double dissociations can be demonstrated (Shallice, 1988). Just such a double dissociation appears in the reports of two separate case studies, one reported by Farah and colleagues, and the other by Hanley et al. (1991).

Farah et al. (1988) described a neuropsychological patient who appeared to have a deficit in the performance of visual imagery tasks, but had spared function for spatial imagery tasks. Patient L.H. had damage to the right temporal lobe and the right inferior frontal lobe, in addition to damage to the temporo-occipital regions on both sides. The visual imagery tasks involved presenting the names of objects or animals about which the patient had to make some judgement based on the visual appearance of the object. Specifically, the tasks involved identifying the characteristic colour of objects, deciding on the relative size of two items that are similar in physical size, judging the length of animals' tails relative to their body size, and judging the similarity in the shapes of states of the USA. The spatial tasks involved mental rotation, mental scanning, Brooks matrix and letter corner tasks (Brooks, 1967; 1968; for a description see Chapter 3), and the locations of states of the USA. Subject L.H. showed significantly poorer performance on all four visual tasks. However he showed performance equivalent to that of controls on all of the spatial tasks, and in some cases (e.g. Brooks letter corner task) L.H. performed better than did control subjects.

Hanley et al. (1991; Hanley, Pearson, & Young, 1990) described a patient who appeared to have the opposite deficit, namely a sparing of visual imagery but with a deficit in spatial processing following a right hemisphere aneurysm. Patient E.L.D. showed poor performance relative to controls on the Brooks matrix task and on Corsi blocks. However she performed well on versions of the four tasks used by Farah et al. (1988) to test visual processing.

Although these two patients provide an apparent double dissociation, the neuroanatomical evidence is less clear, as both L.H. and E.L.D. had right hemisphere lesions, with L.H. having an additional lesion in the posterior left hemisphere. Moreover, E.L.D. has fairly widespread damage across the frontal area of the right hemisphere, and this provides little information as to the neuroanatomical corollaries of her functional impairments.

Other studies have indicated the contrasting result that right anterior temporal damage results in impairments in recognition and recall of photographs of faces, of geometric designs, and of complex visual scenes (Kimura, 1963; Milner, 1968; Pigott & Milner, 1993). The extent of the impairment in each of these studies did not appear to be related to whether or not the hippocampus was damaged. However loss of spatial memory has been shown to be closely linked to hippocampal damage (Corkin, 1965; Milner, 1965, 1971; Petrides, 1985; Pigott & Milner, 1993; Smith & Milner, 1989). For example the recent study by Pigott and Milner (1993) reported visual and spatial memory deficits in a group of 65 patients with right anterior temporal damage. The patients were shown complex visual scenes derived from Mandler and Johnson (1976), and tested for recognition and recall of the figurative details of the objects or for their spatial locations. All of the patients were impaired in their ability to remember details of the visual characteristics of objects in the presented scenes. However only those patients with extensive damage to the hippocampus, or removal of the hippocampus, were impaired in their ability to remember the location of objects in the scene. Pigott and Milner go on to argue that spatial memory depends on an intact hippocampus whereas visual memory appears to rely on the right anterior temporal lobe.

Further evidence from patients has reported that cortical excisions for temporal cortical epilepsy in the right hemisphere impairs spatial memory, but leaves verbal short-term memory intact (Corkin, 1965; Kimura, 1963; Milner, 1965). In other studies of groups of patients, visuo-spatial memory deficits are most frequently associated with lesions in the posterior part of the right hemisphere, specifically in the posterior parietal lobe close to its junction with the occipital lobe (Alajouanine, 1960; Butters, Barton, & Brody, 1970; Warrington & James, 1967). The distinction is also clear when considering the patients described by De Renzi and Nichelli (1975; De Renzi et al., 1977), and by Hanley et al. (1991) all of whom had deficits in the right hemisphere, and all of whom showed deficits of primarily spatial tasks such as the Brooks matrix or the Corsi Blocks. Patients with deficits in retention of primarily visual information such as the Warrington and Rabin (1971) "span of apprehension" test tended to have lesions in the posterior left hemisphere.

VISUAL INFORMATION IN MOVEMENT CONTROL

The discussion of neuropsychological data so far has concentrated on mental representation of visual and/or spatial information. In Chapter 4, the discussion of separate visual and spatial components of working memory led to the association between spatial processing and the control of movement. The argument was based on dual task studies comprising for example some form of spatial processing or spatial memory task, coupled with visual or spatial secondary tasks. The spatial secondary tasks involved arm movement such as tracking a moving target or sequentially tapping an array of unseen switches, while the visual secondary tasks involved brightness judgements (Baddeley & Lieberman, 1980). The primary spatial tasks were disrupted by concurrent movement but were unaffected by concurrent visual processing. In contrast, visual retention tasks were disrupted by secondary visual tasks but not by secondary spatial tasks (Baddeley & Lieberman, 1980; Farmer et al., 1986; Logie, 1986; Logie & Marchetti, 1991). It would be interesting then at this stage to explore whether there are patients with disorders of spatial representation and processing who have spared visual processing and retention functions.

One candidate pattern of impairments has been reported in studies of patients suffering from Optic Ataxia. Patients with this disorder appear to have normal visual acuity and to have normal perception and representation of visual space, but they are unable to use visual information to coordinate their arm movements when reaching out for objects or other visual targets. This is true for both familiar and for unfamiliar targets. For example, when reaching out to grasp an object, the patients initially may open their hand too far and may close their grip prematurely, thereby missing the object completely or knocking it over (Jakobson, Archibald, Carey, & Goodale, 1991; Jeannerod, 1986). Despite this they are unimpaired on general motor ability or strength of grasp, and are able to reach accurately in response to an auditory or kinaesthetic cue. Therefore the inability is in using visual information to guide movement rather than in movement control.

A very clear report of 10 such patients was published by Perenin and Vighetto in 1988. Their patients had lesions in the posterior parietal cortex on either the left or right hemisphere. All the patients appeared able to perceive visual scenes accurately, but were unable to orient their arm movement correctly to visually presented targets when the movement involved the arm contralateral to that of the lesion. When using the arm on the impaired side, the patients made significant errors in reaching for familiar objects such as a large pencil. In another task, the patients were shown circular cards, with a rectangular hole cut out of the middle. Their goal was to reach out and orient their hand so as to place it in the rectangular gap. None of the patients was able to do this successfully with the hand on the side opposite to that of their lesion. In all cases patients made successful targeted movements using the hand that was on the same side as the lesion. Other cases have been reported where the reaching impairment affects both hands in the same patient (e.g. Damasio & Benton, 1979; Rondot, De Recondo, & Ribadeau Dumas, 1977; see also De Renzi, 1982, p.113 ff). In these patients, then, there is evidence that is consistent with a dissociation between visual information about an object and the processing of the spatial information necessary for physically interacting with the object.

VISUO-SPATIAL REPRESENTATIONS
AND NEUROANATOMY

It will be clear from the discussion so far that although there is reasonably strong neuropsychological evidence for a dissociation between visual and spatial short-term memory, there is no clear agreement as to the neuroanatomy that might be linked with this dissociation. Some further clues have been derived from some detailed neuroanatomical studies of non-human primates (Derrington & Lennie, 1984; DeYoe & Van Essen, 1988; Maunsell & Newsome, 1987; Mishkin, Ungerleider, & Macko, 1983; Ungerleider & Mishkin, 1982; Van Essen, Anderson, & Felleman, 1992). The thesis from these studies is that visual information is projected via a common pathway to the occipital lobe in a region of the striatal cortex known as V1. From that point, there are two independent routes, one of which goes via area V5 in the occipital lobe, ending up in the parietal cortex. This dorsal pathway known as the magnocellular or "M" stream appears to deal with object location, or "where" an object is. This pathway appears to be sensitive to low spatial frequencies and has high contrast sensitivity as well as being sensitive to high temporal frequencies. This last property also associates the pathway with the processing of movement. The second, ventral pathway known as the parvocelluar or "P" stream ends up in the temporal cortex via area V4. This pathway is sensitive to high spatial frequencies, to low temporal frequencies, and to spectral information such as colour and shade. This combination of properties is associated with object identification, object form, and object colour, or "what" an object is.

However, despite the initial appeal of the "what" and "where" pathways, the situation is actually rather more complex. Zeki and Shipp (1988) have noted that although area V4 projects to the temporal cortex, it also projects to an area of the parietal cortex. This area is in turn linked to the destination in the parietal cortex of the "where" (V5) route. Similarly V5 projects to both the temporal and the parietal cortex, with subsequent interconnections between the destinations.

We can cope with this further complication by noting that even though visual and spatial information may be handled separately at one level of processing, it is clear that normal subjects can remember the location of particular objects, and at some level of the processing system these two items of information have to be coordinated. For example in following a moving object across the visual scene we are aware of the movement and can retain information about that movement independently of the identity of the moving object. However normal adults are quite capable of associating object identity with object trajectory. For example we can note that we saw a bird or a rugby ball and observe that they followed the same trajectory at different times, but we would not believe that our team had scored if we saw a crow fly between the upright posts on the rugby field! Zeki and Shipp specifically suggest that the scheme of having separate pathways which later converge may be one that is repeated across the cortex, providing the combination of specialised, parallel processing together with coordination of the products of that processing.

A key aspect of representing visual and spatial information is that it cannot of course be entirely dependent on the mapping of object position to retinal coordinates. The eyes move about continuously and rapidly, and yet most of the time we are left with the impression of a stable environment. The repeated fixations of the eyes must feed into some internal representation of the environment, and that representation must incorporate not just visual information, but also information concerned with the relationship of the body to objects in space. There is a large literature on possible neuroanatomical correlates of this representation, some of which I have already described. For example Pigott and Milner (1993) and others have argued that the hippocampus hosts the representation of spatial information.

Stein (1992) has suggested that the parietal cortex, and in particular the posterior parietal cortex, is a much better candidate as a locus for the representation of space in relation to the body, or egocentric space. He argues that the hippocampus appears to deal with information about the spatial relationships among objects in space, but does not incorporate the information about the positions of body parts. He points out that the posterior area of the parietal lobe receives inputs not only from the primary visual cortex via the "what" and "where" pathways as noted by Zeki and Shipp, but also from the auditory system, the proprioceptive system, the vestibular system, and the somatosensory system. Moreover, there are projections to the posterior parietal cortex from areas dealing with information about movement of the eyes, head, limbs, and body. Thus the information that is coordinated in the parietal cortex concerns not only the association between where an object is and what it is, but also the relation between the position and movement of parts of the body and the relative positions of body parts to objects in space.

Stein's views are not wholly new (e.g. De Renzi, 1982) but are still controversial, as is evident from the commentaries that are included in the same issue of the journal in which his article appeared. However his arguments are persuasive and they have considerable appeal for theories of normal cognition that are concerned with mental representation. Moreover, damage to the posterior parietal cortex has also been linked to impairments in visuo-spatial imagery (Bisiach & Luzzatti, 1978; Bisiach et al., 1979). Some researchers are rather less specific, linking visual imagery with the posterior region of the left hemisphere (e.g. Farah, 1984), or with either hemisphere (e.g. Sergent, 1989). What is encouraging is that there appears to be quite strong neuroanatomical evidence for the conflation of several sources of information about egocentric space, and that these sources of information may function more or less independently of one another, until such time as the various information types are brought together.

An interesting corollary of this form of organisation is that the loss of any one source does not cause a complete breakdown of the representation, because other complementary sources are available. So, for example, if purely visual information is unavailable, a sense of egocentric space can be gained from kinaesthetic, auditory, somasthetic, and proprioceptive information. This kind of scenario would readily account for the reports of a form of spatial imagery in the blind (e.g. Cornoldi et al., 1991; Kerr, 1983; Millar, 1990). One argument, then, could be that the visual image is not merely a visual and spatial representation, but also contains information as to some form of egocentric frame of reference.

An emergent consequence of this argument is that it complicates the interpretation of neuropsychological studies. Specifically, when observing a pattern of impairment, there is no guarantee that this pattern arises from the functioning of some global representation that simply has a chunk of missing data from a damaged pathway. The pattern of impairment and sparing might arise from a set of algorithms (or strategies) which attempt to form a functional, global representation derived from the information that is available. So, for example, if the "where" pathway from the visual cortex is damaged, information may reach the posterior parietal cortex via the "what" pathway, and this would be combined with data that were available from tactile, vestibular, and auditory sources. In other words, do the behavioural, neurophysiological, neuroanatomical, and event-related potential data from brain-damaged patients reflect the operation of a damaged system, or of a "coping algorithm" that has arisen in response to the damage? This algorithm may not be evident in normal cognition. Performance of a brain-damaged subject, then, is not simply normal performance that has a bit missing.

Some insight into this problem in theory development can be gained if we return to a section of the article by Stein (1992) where he briefly describes a PDP type model of the functioning of the posterior parietal lobe, and how such a model might account for how a coherent representation of egocentric space could be derived from information from very different sources, and which use different coordinate systems. For example the retinal coordinate system is not entirely linear, with an over-representation of data from the fovea, and under-representation from peripheral vision. The coordinate system based on tactile and proprioceptive input relies on information about the distances between body parts, and their mutual spatial relationships. In essence, his suggestion is that each type of information projected onto the posterior parietal area weights the connections differentially according to the nature of the source, and this allows the PDP network to represent egocentric space topographically. When one information source is damaged, the weights of the connections are then determined by information arriving from intact sources, and a topographic representation can still emerge. It is not as rich a representation, but may be adequate for interacting with objects that are within reach. This demonstrates an attractive feature of PDP networks in that they degrade gracefully rather than catastrophically when they encounter loss of data. The network also degrades gracefully if the damage is to the network rather than to an information source that feeds into the network. Thus a pattern of impairment might arise from damage to the network, or from damage to a pathway that projects to that network. In principle, it might be impossible to tell which bit of the system is damaged by referring to behavioural data. In one sense this makes life difficult for cognitive neuropsychology, but it provides a very neat explanation for why similar patterns of impairment can arise from lesions with very different neuroanatomical locations.

The PDP approach has considerable appeal, but of course does not provide an explanation at a functional, psychological level. In this case, the argument can be translated fairly readily by suggesting that neuropsychological patients may develop strategies to help them cope with their damage. Moreover, different individual patients with the same damage might develop different coping strategies. Thus patterns of sparing and impairment might reflect the nature and efficiency of the coping strategies, and not the nature of the damaged system. It is widely known that normal subjects develop strategies to cope with the requirements of an experimental task (e.g. Della Sala et al., 1991; Siegler, 1987), although this fact is rarely acknowledged in studies of normal cognition (Logie et al., submitted). It is also well known within cognitive neuropsychology that patients develop strategies, but here again, the fact is rarely acknowledged. Caramazza (1986; Caramazza & McCloskey, 1988) has argued that by their very nature, patient groups are rarely homogeneous with respect to their lesion site, even among patients who have apparently the same neuropsychological profile. He points out that group studies of patients are therefore very misleading in that the aggregate data from the group cannot reflect the nature of the damage suffered by any one patient. Moreover, he argues that if the patient group is homogeneous, then there is little point in conducting a group study, because the data pattern from any one patient should reflect the pattern of the group as a whole.

The way forward, according to Caramazza, is to conduct multiple single case-studies of patients, with each patient being the subject of a series of experiments. The cumulative record across patients then provides us with some insight into the disorders. I should like to go further and argue that even when patients have the same lesion site, they may not attempt to cope with their damage in the same way. In addition, some patients may change their strategies from one occasion to another. Therefore in testing any patient there should be measures of test–retest reliability on each test performed, to ensure that the patient is at least performing the test reliably in the same way. By this means we might get some notion as to the pattern of performance that arises when patients use a particular strategy. The hope is that this strategy reliably uses a particular combination of components of the available cognitive architecture.

The issue remains as to whether studies of neuropsychological patients can actually tell us anything at all about normal human cognition. What we end up with is a set of theories about the functioning of damaged systems, and no coherent way to link these to theories of normal cognitive function. The method that best seems to deal with this apparent impasse is to attempt an approach based on converging operations, looking for common conclusions derived from a wide range of data sources rather than relying solely on behavioural, neuropsychological data. This brief review indicates that the neuropsychological data, brain scan data, and event-related potential data, do appear to converge on the main theme of the last two chapters. There does indeed appear to be strong evidence that spatial and visual information are processed separately, but that they are brought together to form some global representation of egocentric space. This global representation does also appear to be available for manipulation in the form of visual images, and there are links between that representation and the planning and control of movement to targets.

This conclusion hints at the functional model, in that visual short-term memory may be considered a separate system from spatial short-term memory, but that both kinds of information are contained in visual images. It provides a basis for the dichotomy between visual and spatial working memory, and for a dissociation between both of these specialist systems and the imagery system. A detailed characterisation of this view is the topic of the final chapter of the book.

CHAPTER SIX

Assumptions, Reconciliation, and Theory Development

There have been three recurrent themes throughout this book. The first focused on the assumption that visuo-spatial working memory and visual imagery cohabit components of the cognitive architecture. The second theme addressed the assumption of a symbiotic relationship between visual and spatial working memory. The third explored the assumption that working memory acts as a gateway to long-term memory. This final chapter provides something of a reprise with variations on these themes, and some further evidence for a modified view of how working memory might host these related cognitive functions.

I have argued that the term visuo-spatial working memory describes not a single system, but a set of distinct cognitive functions each of which relies on separate components of the cognitive architecture. The orchestrated use of these components supports the retention and processing of visual and spatial information. The generation and manipulation of conscious visual images relies on executive functions, while separate temporary stores are charged with the retention respectively of spatial material and of visual material. Finally, access to these functions occurs only via long-term memory representations.

The distinction between visual and spatial working memory stems from the dual task studies discussed in Chapter 4, and from the neuropsychological evidence in Chapter 5. Although it is not firmly established, there is now a reasonably wide range of evidence to support the distinction. The divorce of visual and spatial storage from visual imagery has only limited support from the data considered so far. The structure of this chapter, then, is first to explore some further evidence for the visual/spatial distinction, and for the link between spatial working memory and movement. Second, I shall discuss some recent data that speaks to the link between executive functions and visual imagery. In the final part of the chapter, I shall flesh out some of the details and implications of the modifications to the working memory model (see Fig. 6.6, p.127) that emerge from these findings, and from the theoretical re-routing of sensory input.

SPATIAL REPRESENTATION AND
MOVEMENT CONTROL

The experiments by Baddeley and Lieberman (1980), Logie and Marchetti (1991), by Quinn (1988; 1991; Quinn & Ralston, 1986), and by Smyth (Smyth & Pendleton, 1989) among others, all pointed to the suggestion that the retention of spatial information, the retention of movements, and the production of movements relied on overlapping cognitive resources. Moreover the data on optic ataxia, and on neuroanatomical mapping discussed in Chapter 5 indicated that spatial representation and movement control relied on similar neuroanatomical structures and pathways, most notably, the hippocampus, the parietal lobe, and the dorsal pathway or magnocellular stream from the primary visual areas of the occipital lobe to the parietal cortex.

Additional supportive evidence for this spatial/movement link comes from studies of normal movement control. It is clear that much of movement planning requires the use of visual feedback (e.g. Thomson, 1986). Moving one's hand to a target requires accurate information about the location of the target with respect to the initial position of the hand and arm. From studies of arm movements, it has been observed that the trajectory taken by the arm during a movement is closely related to an overall motor plan that is based on precise information about the position of a target object. The trajectory is much less determined by motor control at the level of the detailed movements of the joints and muscles. For example if the arm is loaded with a weight, unless the weight is excessive the arm follows a trajectory to the target that is almost identical to that followed when no extra weight is present. This is true even though the demand on the muscles of the arm is significantly different in the two cases (see e.g. Bernstein, 1967; Hollerbach, 1990). That is, within limits, the muscles can compensate for the additional strain and execute the trajectory planned by higher-level control functions. These control functions use visual feedback to generate a spatial representation of the position of the hand and arm in relation to the target. (See also Bizzi & Mussa-Ivaldi, 1990; Mussa-Ivaldi, 1988).

At a neurophysiological level, Georgopoulos, Kalaska, Caminiti, and Massey (1982; 1983) have shown a correlation between the direction of movement to a target, and the activity of particular neurons in the parietal cortex of monkeys. This finding can be coupled with the report by Anderson Essick, and Siegel (1987) that the parietal cortex is responsible for transforming the retinal image of an object into a representation of where that object is in relation to the eyes, and subsequently to the body. A similar argument was put forward by Stein (1992) whose work was discussed in Chapter 5. This pattern of results is consistent with the view that neural activity related to motor planning (but not the overt production of the movement itself), is associated with neural activity that is implicated in forming representations of the location of objects in space.

This line of argument fits very neatly with the findings from the experiments by Baddeley and Lieberman, by Quinn, by Smyth, and by Logie and Marchetti, which demonstrated a close link between the cognitive activities involved in representing movements in space, and those involved in movement. From the neurophysiological and neuro-psychological data, it appears that it is the planning of the arm movement rather than the movement itself which seems to be important. For example Quinn (1994) has found that when movements of the arm are passive (the experimenter holds and moves the subject's arm for them), and are random (so that the subjects cannot predict where their arm is moving to next), then no disruption of Brooks (1967) matrix task performance is observed. Interference does occur when subjects generate movements themselves, or where the experimenter moves their arm and subjects can predict where their arm is being led. In other words when subjects do not plan the movement of their arm, they can retain the Brooks matrix material with impunity. Cognitive conflicts with matrix generation and retention arise only when the subject actively plans and/or executes the movement.

Some further unpublished data collected by Idzikowski and colleagues (cited in Baddeley, 1986) suggest that active movement of the eyes may also be implicated. In this experiment, subjects were required to perform the Brooks matrix task in two eye-movement conditions. In one condition, the eye movements were passive. This was achieved by spinning the subject around in a revolving chair, a procedure that results in involuntary eye movements, referred to as post-rotational nystagmus. In the complement-ary condition, subjects were required to follow with their eyes a target on a computer screen which moved gradually down the screen while swinging back and forth in a sinusoidal fashion. The active eye movement required for following the moving target disrupted performance of the spatial imagery task, but the involuntary eye movements had no effect on performance.

Thus the link between spatial representation and motor control seems quite close. One way in which this system might work is for a visual representation system to hold information about a visual scene and a potential target. The information about the location of a target item in the scene is then extracted from the visual representation, and this information feeds into the planning of movement to a target in the scene. Thus the movement planning system acts in partnership with the visual representational system, but nevertheless they comprise separate mechanisms. This view of course predicts that we should find evidence that movements which involve a target might be distinguished from movements which do not. Such evidence has indeed been reported. For example Smyth and Pendleton (1989) demonstrated that retention of arm movement configurations (e.g. moving the arm in a circle, or clenching the fist) is not disrupted by moving the arm to a series of targets during a retention interval. This, together with the evidence discussed earlier lends added support to the idea that movement planning can be distinct from representation of an object (see also Marteniuk, 1976; Posner, 1967), but that when movement to a target is required, the movement planning system and the object representation system act in concert.

VISUAL IMAGERY AND WORKING MEMORY

In Chapter 4, I discussed the data from Alice Salway's experiments which coupled the Brooks matrix task and the Brooks verbal task with concurrent random generation. You may recall that random generation appeared to affect the Brooks matrix task rather more than it affected the verbal task, suggesting that of the two, the matrix task appears to impose a larger load on the central executive of working memory. This load is in addition to any specific demands placed on visuo-spatial resources. The Space Fortress experiments reported by Logie et al. (1989; see also Fabiani et al., 1989) came to a similar conclusion about the executive load imposed by the Brooks tasks.

Salway also explored the effect of secondary tasks on a more traditional mental imagery task, namely mental rotation (Logie & Salway, 1990; Salway, 1991). She took as her main task, the mental rotation of abstract shapes employed by Cooper (1975; Cooper & Podgorny, 1976). This involved presenting subjects with a "standard" shape, followed by an orientation arrow. This display then disappeared to be replaced with a comparison shape which was in the same orientation as the arrow shown previously. The comparison shape was either identical to the standard, was a modified shape, or was a mirror image, and decision times and errors were recorded. Examples of the stimuli used are shown in Fig. 6.1.

The mental rotation task was either performed on its own, or was combined with one of a number of secondary tasks, namely articulatory suppression (saying "go-go-go"), oral random generation of digits from the

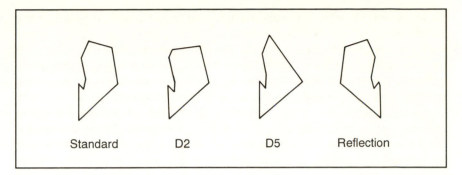

FIG. 6.1. Example of the stimuli used in the Logie and Salway (1990) mental rotation study.

set zero to nine, spatial tapping of four switches arranged in a square, and repeated tapping of a single switch. Figure 6.2 shows some of the data from this experiment in terms of the percentage change from control performance in each of the secondary task conditions. In the graph, control performance is shown as 100%, and it is clear that neither tapping a single switch, nor articulatory suppression had any effect on the mental rotation task. In contrast, spatial suppression caused a significant drop in

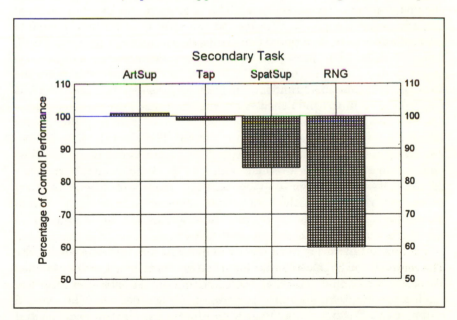

FIG. 6.2. Performance on the mental rotation task when performed alone and when performed concurrently with secondary tasks. Data from Logie and Salway (1990).

performance, whereas oral random generation resulted in an even larger decrement.

This experiment, then, appears to support the involvement of visuo-spatial working memory, and indicates that very little if any phonological storage was required. Oral random generation is assumed to place a load on the central executive in addition to its similarity to articulatory suppression, and from these data it is clear that the effects of random generation are not due to its reliance on spoken output. That is, the mental rotation task appears to rely heavily on executive resources as well as on visuo-spatial resources, but with verbal working memory making little or no contribution.

There is some further, recent, as yet unpublished data (Logie, in prep.) from dual task experiments carried out by myself and colleagues in Aberdeen which speak to the executive role in the mental discovery tasks discussed in Chapter 2. You may recall that one particular task originally reported by Finke and Slayton (1988) involved presenting subjects with the names of letters. The letters had to be imaged and mentally manipulated according to verbal instructions, and the subject then had to report a name for the resulting image. Example stimuli from the new dual task experiment are shown in Fig. 6.3. In this study subjects were required to perform the imagery manipulation task on its own or concurrently with one of a number of secondary tasks. The secondary tasks were as follows: (1) articulatory suppression (repeating the word "the"); (2) oral random generation of digits; (3) tapping four switches arranged in a square pattern; and (4) random key pressing. In this last task subjects were given a specially constructed keyboard with 10 keys, and were asked to press the keys one at a time in as random a fashion as possible. This last task has not been used in the published literature, and was intended to act as a non-verbal equivalent to oral random generation for loading the central executive (Baddeley, personal communication). The mental discovery task itself was assessed by asking subjects first to produce a name for their image, and second to draw their image on paper. The names and the drawings were then given to independent judges to assess whether they adequately represented the figure that should result from the verbal instructions. The judges were not informed as to the experimental conditions from which the data were derived.

The mental discovery task clearly relies both on verbal input for the instructions, and on imagery manipulation in response to the instructions. Therefore we should find that both articulatory suppression and oral random generation disrupt performance, because of the verbal requirement. Further if the imagery manipulation relies on visuo-spatial working memory, we should find that tapping in a square should disrupt performance (e.g. Farmer et al., 1986). The random key pressing should

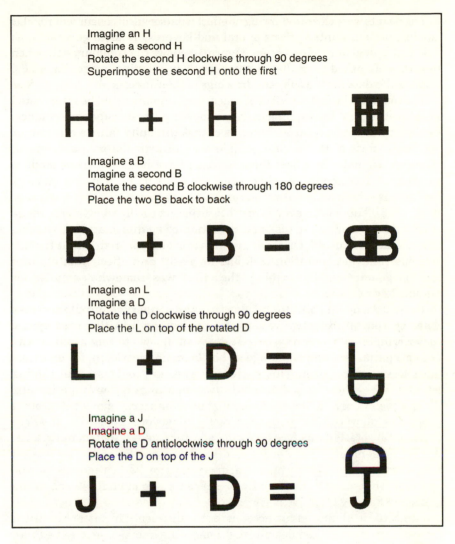

FIG. 6.3. Example stimuli used in the Logie (in prep.) study.

have similar effects to that of regular tapping. However if the central executive is responsible for imagery manipulation then concurrent regular tapping would not interfere, but random tapping might do so because of its assumed additional executive loading. The central executive hypothesis would also predict disruption from oral random generation, and we would expect interference with the verbal retention of the instructions by both random generation and articulatory suppression.

The results were clear in showing no effect whatsoever of concurrent regular tapping, but substantial effects of oral and keypress random generation as well as of articulatory suppression. Figure 6.4 shows the summary data when subjects were asked to produce a name for their resulting image. Figure 6.5 displays the data for the subjects' drawings of their images.

The complete lack of an effect of concurrent tapping could be interpreted as suggesting that the tapping task was too simple to disrupt performance. However, this interpretation in terms of task difficulty fails to account for the large effect of the equally simple task of articulatory suppression. Moreover virtually identical tapping tasks have been shown to produce substantial decrements in other forms of visuo-spatial working memory functioning where articulatory suppression has had no effect (e.g. Farmer et al., 1986). There is an even larger literature on the link between a range of concurrent movement tasks on retention of spatial material, which I have already discussed. On these grounds it is also surprising that the key pressing random generation task had no greater an effect than did oral random generation. If anything, the effect was somewhat smaller for random key pressing.

These data again point to the idea that the imagery manipulation task relies on central executive resources, supplemented in this case by the verbal temporary storage system. It does not appear to rely at all on any form of spatial temporary storage as has been implicated in, for example, the Brooks matrix task. This pattern of results provides an intriguing contrast with those found for Salway's mental rotation experiments. Clearly the Finke and Slayton task must use some form of mental rotation in order to follow the instructions correctly. However it appears that where this mental rotation involves following auditory, verbal instructions, as in the experiment just described, there is little need for visual or spatial temporary *storage*. This form of temporary storage did however seem to be required for retaining the visually presented abstract shapes used in the Logie and Salway (1990) experiment.

If this last explanation can account for the difference in pattern between the two experiments just described, it leaves the question as to why there is such widespread evidence for spatial storage in the case of the Brooks matrix task. In this case, there is verbal, auditory input of instructions with subjects required to form an image based on those instructions. It is possible to account for this seeming anomaly if we consider that the Brooks task requires temporary storage of the path around the matrix. In the Logie and Salway experiment, there is also a requirement to store the exact form of the standard shape in order to make a comparison with a subsequently presented shape. In the mental discovery experiment, there is not the same pressing need for storage of the exact visual or the spatial properties of the stimuli. The presented letters can be regenerated from long-term memory,

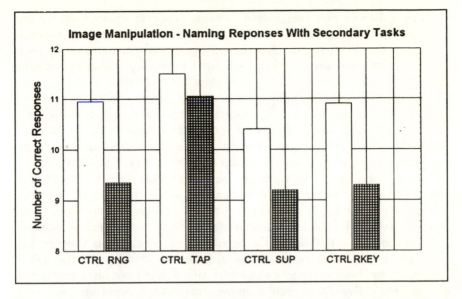

FIG. 6.4. Summary data when subjects are asked to produce a name for a resultant image with and without a concurrent secondary task.

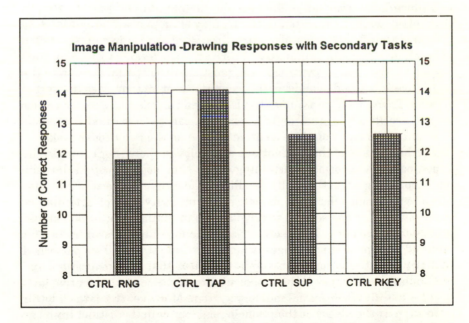

FIG. 6.5. Summary data when subjects are asked to produce a drawing of a resultant image with and without a concurrent secondary task.

and storage could be accomplished by rehearsing the instructions rather than by maintaining a visual image. Therefore in the Finke and Slayton procedure, we could conclude that there is a processing demand for imagery manipulation but there is no requirement for temporary visual or spatial storage.

Further hints about the importance of the central executive in imagery and in the Brooks tasks in particular come from one of the neuro-psychological studies described in Chapter 5. The patient E.L.D. described by Hanley et al. (1991) appeared to have difficulty with retaining spatial material coupled with a relatively intact ability to retain, and have access to, visual information. This pattern was contrasted with a patient who appeared to have the opposite disorder, namely an impairment of visual storage and processing, but intact spatial ability. This contrast was consistent with the visual versus spatial distinction in working memory, but the contrast is perhaps not as straightforward as it might seem. On closer inspection it was noticeable that E.L.D. had difficulty with the verbal version of the Brooks task as well as with the matrix task. She could recall only two out of five of the verbal sequences correctly. Normal adult subjects in the Baddeley and Lieberman (1980) study successfully recalled 6.5 sequences out 8 in the control condition. Clearly it would have been ideal to have data from normal subjects who were matched with E.L.D. on age and educational level, but unfortunately the control data from the Brooks verbal task were not reported in the Hanley et al. paper. The spatial data indicated that E.L.D. was indeed impaired on that task in that she failed to recall any of the matrix patterns correctly. However, as I have argued earlier, there is strong evidence to suggest that the spatial version of the task places greater demands on the executive system than does the verbal version. Therefore if we assume that E.L.D. had an executive deficit rather than a specifically spatial deficit, her data can be accounted for by the differential demands on the executive by each of the two Brooks tasks.

Further details of this patient are also relevant here. For example she appeared to have normal functioning of the phonological loop in that she had a normal span, successfully recalling sequences of six letters. She also exhibited normal effects of phonological similarity and of articulatory suppression, and she seemed to have access to spatial information stored in long-term memory. On the other hand she failed to perform tasks that involved manipulation of images, such as mental rotation. This pattern of findings is entirely consistent with the view that the generation and manipulation of images is the responsibility of the central executive, and not of a specific visuo-spatial memory system. Moreover the data on letter span support the idea that the phonological loop is quite distinct from the two sets of cognitive functions underlying respectively visual imagery and visuo-spatial temporary memory.

A differing approach to this issue is to consider whether individual differences in performance of central executive tasks correlate with individual abilities on imagery manipulation tasks. One such source of evidence is a study by Salthouse, Mitchell, Skovronek, and Babcock (1989) who were investigating the claims that working memory is rather less effective in the healthy elderly than it is in the young. Their assumed view was of working memory as a single flexible resource (see Chapter 1), and they measured cognitive abilities in three different ways. The first of these was a verbal reasoning task with problems like the following:

K and F do the opposite
H and K do the same
If H decreases what will happen to F?

The second task involved mental paper folding where subjects were shown a sequence of paper folds and they were then asked whether a target pattern would match the outcome of the paper-folding sequence.

The third task was thought to be a measure of working memory capacity and involved a series of simple sums, followed by a request to recall some of the numbers presented as part of each sum, for example:

4 + 3 = ?
9 − 4 = ?
5 + 2 = ?
7 − 1 = ?

Subjects would then have to recall the second number from each sum, which in this case would be 3-4-2-1. The number of sums was increased until subjects could no longer accurately recall the sequence of numbers, thereby proffering a measure that Salthouse et al. referred to as a computational span. This last task was thought to be equivalent to the Daneman and Carpenter (1980) sentence span task, incorporating on-line processing with temporary storage. As you may recall from Chapter 1 the suggestion is that individuals who do well on these kinds of tasks have a high working memory capacity and can cope with a larger number of items for storage despite the ongoing processing load. Moreover, as noted before, Just and Carpenter (1992) suggested that their notion of working memory (and *ipso facto* the Salthouse et al. view of working memory) probably overlaps substantially with the concept of a central executive in the Baddeley and Hitch model (see also Baddeley et al., 1985). On these grounds then, the computational span could be considered as a measure of executive loading, although it is likely that some form of phonological storage is required in addition.

In a group of 120 adults, drawn from a wide age range, Salthouse and his colleagues found that paper folding and verbal reasoning correlated quite highly with one another (0.62), and both correlated with computational span (0.48 for reasoning, 0.38 for paper folding). All three tasks also correlated negatively with age. However when Salthouse et al. partialled out the influence of the working memory capacity task (computational span), the correlation was greatly reduced between age and performance of the other two tasks.

Therefore, a verbal reasoning task that would presumably rely heavily on central executive resources appears to correlate with performance on a mental imagery manipulation task, and both of these tasks correlate with what has been described as a measure of working memory capacity. These data, then, are entirely consistent with a key role for a general-purpose central executive resource in imagery manipulation tasks.

A MODIFIED VIEW OF VISUO-SPATIAL WORKING MEMORY

If we now consider the relationship between these arguments and theories of visual imagery, a rather different picture emerges of working memory, and in particular of visuo-spatial working memory, than has been assumed in imagery research or in the working memory literature. A schematic diagram of the modified model is shown in Fig. 6.6. In summary, the modified view of visuo-spatial working memory is of a system that comprises a visual temporary store and a spatial temporary store. The route from visual input to both stores is via long-term memory representations of the visual form of objects or the spatial information about a dynamic scene. When these long-term memory representations are activated, the information enters the visual or the spatial part of the system. Which system it enters is determined by the nature of the information activated. The visual store is subject to decay and to interference from new information coming in. The spatial store is seen as a system that can be used to plan movement, but can also be used to rehearse the contents of the visual store. In so doing the spatial system can extract information from the visual store to allow for targeted movement.

The link with visual imagery is that the spatial and visual components provide temporary storage of information from which the central executive can extract material that is relevant to the task in hand. The executive can also access semantic information activated from long-term memory, and can retrieve phonological and articulatory information being held temporarily in the phonological loop.

The idea that the contents of working memory are derived from the activation of long-term memory representations is the basis for a number

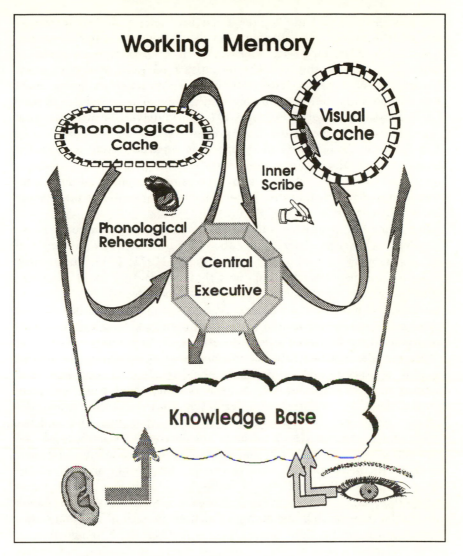

FIG. 6.6. A schematic diagram of the modified model of working memory.

of alternative models of working memory (e.g. Cowan, 1988, 1993; Hasher & Zacks, 1988; Norman, 1968). However, in these models the suggestion is that the contents of working memory essentially *are* the activated long-term memory traces. These authors have less enthusiasm for a set of separate temporary stores to which information about the activated traces is transferred. The case for a separate short-term memory system was argued in some detail in Chapter 1, paving the way for a bifurcation between the cognitive mechanisms involved in short-term storage and those involved in long-term storage, with bi-directional transfer of information between the two. The tentative model proposed here, then, combines the explanatory power of both the "activated traces" view and of the multiple component working memory system. The model is tentative in so far as the purpose of this essay is to elucidate visuo-spatial working memory, and not to constitute a comprehensive case for a general theory of memory. But of necessity the proposal of separate visual and spatial short-term retention systems assumes a separation between a multiple component short-term storage and processing system, and long-term storage functions. The tentative general model is presented to make these assumptions explicit.

Returning specifically to visuo-spatial working memory, there is a sense in which the emerging conclusions about the link between imagery and working memory is reminiscent of the Paivio (1971; 1986) dual coding model of imagery. Paivio's thesis was that information could be stored either visually or verbally, and that these two codes together could lead to better retention than one code alone. At first sight it appears that Paivio's verbal code could be associated with the phonological loop and his visual code could be reinterpreted as visuo-spatial working memory. In addition, a recurrent leitmotif in this volume has been that representations in working memory comprise information held in all three components of working memory, together with information activated from long-term storage. That is, retention of information may be better when the representation includes material held in the phonological loop and the visual and spatial stores. This adds considerable redundancy to the information held and makes it less resistant to loss due to interference or decay. Where the Paivio model and the modified model of working memory part company is in the suggestion that the phonological loop and the visual and spatial components are primarily stores rather than processors. Paivio includes both processing and storage functions in each of his dual codes. Moreover, within Paivio's model, the generation of an image from a presented word requires access to the word's semantics, not to its phonology. In working memory, semantic information is if anything entertained by the central executive, and not by the phonological loop. Similarly, according to the arguments given here, generation of an image appears to be the prerogative of the central executive, while short-term retention of the visual or spatial properties of that image may be the responsibility of the temporary stores that are most appropriate for those properties. Therefore the dual coding model bears only a superficial resemblance to either the form of working memory described by Baddeley (1986) or to the modified form of the model proposed here.

Although Paivio's work was seminal in imagery research, the imagery literature over the last decade has of course been dominated more by Kosslyn's model rather than by dual coding theory. In his model, Kosslyn (1980) described the concept of a visual buffer which acted as host for the consciously experienced image. The buffer was thought to place limitations on the resolution of the image it contained, and to have a foveal-like area which was of a higher resolution and which was linked to the area of attentional focus. He proposed in addition that a number of processes could operate on the contents of buffer. These include: Scan, where the focus of attention shifts to another part of the image; Pan and Zoom which were analogous to "viewing the image" respectively from further away to take in more of the periphery, or from close up to examine detail; and Rotate which allowed manipulation of the orientation of the scene or object portrayed in the image. There were also Generate and Regenerate functions which allowed initial construction of the image, and refreshing of the image or redrawing it in a different form to include new information or to exclude information. Kosslyn has been successful in implementing this model as a computer simulation (see e.g., Kosslyn, 1987, 1991; Kosslyn et al., 1992) and he and his collaborators have described neuropsychological evidence to support its characteristics (e.g. Farah, 1984, 1988; Kosslyn, 1991; Kosslyn, Flynn, Amsterdam, & Wang, 1990).

Is there potential here for an overlap with the concept of working memory? The main thrust of the argument thus far has been that the executive is responsible for imagery generation and manipulation, and one approach would be to suggest that the central executive hosts the visual buffer and controls the operations that act on its contents. According to this view, Kosslyn's visual buffer contains the conscious image which includes the visual properties of the image and the information about the relative location of objects to one another plus any semantic information associated with the image. In this sense it is more like a workspace for visual imagery than a buffer as such. The visual store provides a kind of cache memory for information which may be readily brought into the conscious image for manipulation and inspection. That is, the visual cache contains more visual information than does the conscious image, and information is exchanged between the respective systems.

Kosslyn's processes acting on the contents of the buffer such as Pan, Zoom, Scan, Generate, and Regenerate could be seen as procedures activated from long-term memory and available to the central executive along with a wide range of other algorithms and heuristics for processing information. The Generate/Regenerate functions provide a means to rehearse and refresh the contents of the buffer. One characteristic of the generate/regenerate processes is that they are sequential with the various parts of the image generated in a particular order (Kosslyn et al. 1988; for a discussion see Chapter 2). An emergent property of such a sequential process is that it could retain movement sequences. This point is illustrated by the Logie and Marchetti (1991) study described in Chapter 4. In one condition of this study subjects had to retain the sequential order of presentation of a series of coloured patches which appeared randomly on a computer screen. The presentation order could be retained by mentally drawing and regenerating an image with the squares refreshed in the image in the order in which they had originally appeared. In that study, concurrent movement during the retention interval disrupted recognition memory for the presentation sequence. This account of the generate/ regenerate function is entirely consistent with the arguments in Chapters 4, 5, and earlier in this chapter about the relationship between movement planning and temporary retention of spatial information.

Therefore something akin to Kosslyn's visual buffer embodies the current conscious visual image which may be manipulated by invoking one or more procedures that are appropriate for processing visual images. The visual cache would then provide temporary storage of information as required, and generating and regenerating an image provides a rehearsal function which refreshes the contents of the visual cache and of the visual buffer. An emergent property of this rehearsal function is that it can represent movement. Planning of movement can then be accomplished by running through imagery-based simulations in advance of executing the movement. These simulations are probably not required for highly practised movements and actions but would be useful when preparing for some unpractised or complex movement. For example, there is a large body of evidence suggesting that mental practice of movements can result in better physical performance of those movements by athletes and in a variety of sporting activities such as golf or tennis (e.g. Annett, 1988, 1991; Epstein, 1980; Ungerleider & Golding, 1991; Washburn, 1916).

This mental enactment has effects on memory as well as on overt production of action. For example, Engelkamp (1991; Engelkamp, Zimmer, & Denis, 1989) has shown that requiring someone to imagine themselves miming an action presented as a verbal phrase (e.g. smoking a pipe, throwing a ball) results in better recall for the verbal phrase than does simply generating a static image of the meaning of the phrase (e.g. someone smoking a pipe, or a hand poised to throw a ball). It is as if the mental enactment invokes the operation of processes that allow learning to occur in a way that generating a static image does not. Insofar as enactment involves processing the image dynamically in the central executive, this supports the role of the executive in long-term learning (Baddeley et al., 1984).

Returning, then, to a possible link with the visual buffer, Kosslyn has briefly mentioned a role for working memory in his own model (Kosslyn,

1991, pp.375–376). Working memory is involved in transferring information to and from long-term representations and the visual buffer. That role is entirely consistent with the model described here. However he also equates the visual buffer with short-term visual memory, whereas I would argue that temporary visual storage is a back-up store on which the conscious visual image (the contents of Kosslyn's visual buffer) relies.

VISUO-SPATIAL WORKING MEMORY AND COGNITIVE ARCHITECTURE

I should like to draw the discussion to a close by speculating a little on the implications that the arguments put forward in this essay have for working memory as a concept, for the central executive and particularly for visuo-spatial working memory. The central executive component of working memory has been much maligned, being described variously as a conceptual ragbag, or as an area of residual ignorance, or as a scheduler for allocating attention (Baddeley, 1986), or as a flexible resource that can be used for storage and for processing (Baddeley, 1986; Just & Carpenter, 1992). I should like to suggest that the last of these probably captures the spirit of its function, with the central executive acting as a form of flexible processing "neuroware" which can run a variety of software including the generation and manipulation of visual imagery as well as language comprehension and heuristics for problem solving. It is supported by storage mechanisms, specifically a visual cache and a verbal cache, each of which offers temporary retention of material that is required in on-line processing in the executive. The caches allow us to lay information to one side and return to it a few seconds later after processing segments of the information that are in the conscious image. Moreover we can implement relatively automated procedures such as regenerating or subvocally rehearsing to assist each cache to maintain its contents.

Thus when exploring the nature of cognitive architecture, we can think of the endeavour as addressing the flexible system, or alternatively as addressing the procedures which run on that system. The nature of the flexible system could in principle be characteristic of all neurologically healthy adults. The nature of the procedures could differ dramatically depending on each individual's available knowledge base or their repertoire of procedures, algorithms, and heuristics. Subjects, we know, are strategic, and not all subjects will necessarily attempt to perform the same task using the same components of their neuroware (Della Sala et al, 1991; Logie et al., submitted; see also discussions on strategy in Chapter 2 and Chapter 5). For these reasons an investigation of the individual vagaries of strategy choice might be a useful routine addition to the experimenter's tool kit.

Therefore we can have a theory of the cognitive architecture or we can develop a range of theories about how that cognitive architecture is employed when people accomplish tasks in everyday life or in a laboratory. The thesis of this volume is of working memory as a cognitive architecture comprising a central executive and cache memories, with visual imagery seen as a suite of programs which can be implemented on that architecture. During pursuit of that thesis, this essay has offered a means to build on an existing corpus of knowledge by positive critiqueing rather than by adopting an adversarial approach to the characterisation of the cognitive software and of the cognitive architecture, and in so doing to demonstrate how diverse findings from diverse approaches can allow convergence on a coherent framework for studying both.

References

Alajouanine, T. (1960). *Les grandes activités du lobe occipital*. Paris: Masson.

Anderson, J.H. (1978). Arguments concerning representations for mental imagery. *Psychological Review*, *85*, 249–277.

Anderson, R.A., Essick, G.K., & Siegel, R.M. (1987). Neurons of Area 7 activated by both visual stimuli and oculomotor behavior. *Experimental Brain Research*, *67*, 316–322.

Annett, J. (1988). Imagery and skill acquisition. In M. Denis, J. Engelkamp, & J.T.E. Richardson (Eds.), *Cognitive and neuropsychological approaches to mental imagery*. Amsterdam: Martinus Nijhoff, BV.

Annett, J. (1991). Skill acquisition, In J.E. Morrison (Ed.), *Training for performance: Principles of applied human learning*, pp.13–51. Chichester: Wiley.

Ashcraft, M.H. (1992). Cognitive arithmetic: A review of data and theory. *Cognition*, *44*, 75–106.

Atkinson, R.C., & Shiffrin R.M. (1968). Human memory. A proposed system and its control processes. In K.W. Spence & J.T. Spence (Eds.), *The psychology of learning and motivation* Vol. 2, pp. 89–105. New York: Academic Press.

Atkinson, R.C., & Shiffrin, R.M. (1971). The control of short-term memory. *Scientific American*, *225*, 82–90.

Avons, S.E., & Phillips, W.A. (1987). Representation of matrix patterns in long- and short-term visual memory. *Acta Psychologica*, *65*, 227–246.

Baddeley, A.D. (1966a). Short-term memory for word sequences as a function of acoustic, semantic, and formal similarity. *Quarterly Journal of Experimental Psychology*, *18*, 362–365.

Baddeley, A.D. (1966b). The influence of acoustic and semantic similarity on long-term memory for word sequences. *Quarterly Journal of Experimental Psychology*, *18*, 302–309.

Baddeley, A.D. (1966c). The capacity for generating information by randomization. *Quarterly Journal of Experimental Psychology, 18,* 1 19–130.

Baddeley, A.D. (1968). A three minute reasoning test based on grammatical transformation. *Psychonomic Science, 10,* 341–342.

Baddeley, A.D. (1986). *Working memory.* Oxford: Oxford University Press.

Baddeley, A.D. (1990). *Human memory: Theory and practice.* Hove, UK: Lawrence Erlbaum Associates Ltd.

Baddeley, A.D. (1992). Is working memory working? The fifteenth Bartlett Lecture. *Quarterly Journal of Experimental Psychology, 44,* 1–31.

Baddeley, A.D., Bressi, S., Della Sala, S., Logie, R.H., & Spinnler, H. (1991). The decline of working memory in Alzheimer's disease: A longitudinal study. *Brain, 114,* 2521–2542.

Baddeley, A.D., Della Sala, S., & Spinnler, H. (1991). The two-component hypothesis of memory deficit in Alzheimer's disease. *Journal of Clinical and Experimental Neuropsychology, 13,* 372–380.

Baddeley, A.D., Grant, W., Wight, E., & Thomson, N. (1975b). Imagery and visual working memory. In P.M.A. Rabbitt & S. Dornic (Eds.), *Attention and performance V,* pp.205–217. London: Academic Press.

Baddeley, A.D., & Hitch, G.J., (1974). Working memory. In G. Bower (Ed.), *The psychology of learning and motivation, Vol. VIII,* pp.47–90, New York: Academic Press.

Baddeley, A.D., & Hitch G.J. (1977). Recency re-examined. In S. Donic (Ed.), *Attention and performance,* Vol. 6, pp. 647–667. Hillsdale, NJ: Lawrence Erlbaum Associates Inc.

Baddeley, A.D., & Hitch G.J. (1993). The recency effect: Implicit learning with explicit retrieval. *Memory and Cognition, 21,* 146–155.

Baddeley, A.D., & Lewis, V.J. (1981). Inner active processes in reading: The inner voice, the inner ear and the inner eye. In A.M. Lesgold & C.A. Perfetti (Eds.), *Interactive processes in reading,* pp.107–129. Hillsdale, NJ: Lawrence Erlbaum Associates Inc.

Baddeley, A.D., Lewis, V.J., Eldridge, M., & Thomson, N. (1984). Attention and retrieval from long-term memory. *Journal of Experimental Psychology: General, 113,* 518–540.

Baddeley, A.D., Lewis, V.J., & Vallar, G. (1984). Exploring the articulatory loop. *Quarterly Journal of Experimental Psychology, 36,* 233–252.

Baddeley, A.D., & Lieberman, K. (1980). Spatial working memory. In R.S. Nickerson (Ed.), *Attention and performance VIII,* pp.521–539, Hillsdale, NJ: Lawrence Erlbaum Associates Inc.

Baddeley, A.D., & Logie, R.H. (1992). Auditory imagery and working memory. In D. Reisberg (Ed.), *Auditory imagery,* pp. 179–197. Hillsdale, NJ: Lawrence Erlbaum Associates Inc.

Baddeley, A.D., Logie, R.H., Bressi, S., Della Sala, S., & Spinnler, H. (1986). Senile dementia and working memory. *Quarterly Journal of Experimental Psychology 38*A, 603–618.

Baddeley, A.D., Logie, R.H., Nimmo-Smith, I., & Brereton, N. (1985). Components of fluent reading. *Journal of Memory and Language, 24,* 119–131.

Baddeley, A.D., Papagno, C., & Vallar, G. (1988). When long-term learning depends on short-term storage. *Journal of Memory and Language, 27,* 586–595.

Baddeley, A.D., Thomson, N., & Buchanan, M. (1975a). Word length and the structure of short-term memory. *Journal of Verbal Learning and Verbal Behavior, 14,* 575–589.

Banks, W.P. (1977). Encoding and processing of symbolic information in comparative judgments. *Psychology of Learning and Motivation, 11,* 101–159.

Banks, W.P., & Flora, J. (1977). Semantic and perceptual processes in symbolic comparisons. *Journal of Experimental Psychology: Human Perception and Performance, 3,* 278–290.

Banks, W.P., Fujii, M., & Kayra-Stuart, F. (1976). Semantic congruity effects in comparative judgments of magnitudes of digits. *Journal of Experimental Psychology: Human Perception and Performance, 2*(3), 435–447.

Barrett, S.E., Rugg, M.D., & Perrett, D.I. (1988). Event-related potentials and the matching of familiar and unfamiliar faces. *Neuropsychologia, 26,* 105–117.

Basso, A., Spinnler, H., Vallar, G., & Zanobio, E. (1982). Left hemisphere damage and selective impairment of auditory verbal short-term memory: A case study. *Neuropsychologia, 20,* 263–274.

Begg, I., & Paivio, A. (1969). Concreteness and imagery in sentence meaning. *Journal of Verbal Learning and Verbal Behavior, 8,* 821–827.

Benson, A.J., & Gedye, J.L. (1963). Logical processes in the resolution of orientational conflict. *RAF Institute of Aviation Medicine Report 259.* Farnborough, UK.

Bernstein, N. (1967). *The coordination and regulation of movements.* Oxford: Pergamon Press.

Besner, D. (1987). Phonology, lexical access in reading, and articulatory suppression: A critical review. *Quarterly Journal of Experimental Psychology, 39*A, 467–478.

Beyn, E.S., & Knyazeva, G.R. (1962). The problem of protoagnosia. *Journal of Neurology, Neurosurgery and Psychiatry, 25,* 154–158.

Bishop, D., & Robson, J. (1989). Unimpaired short-term memory and rhyme judgement in congenitally speechless individuals: Implications for the notion of "articulatory coding". *Quarterly Journal of Experimental Psychology, 41*A, 123–141.

Bisiach. E. (1993). Mental representation in unilateral neglect and related disorders: The twentieth Bartlett memorial lecture. *Quarterly Journal of Experimental Psychology, 46*A, 435–461.

Bisiach, E., & Luzzatti, C. (1978). Unilateral neglect of representational space. *Cortex, 14,* 129–133.

Bisiach, E., Luzzatti, C., & Perani, D. (1979). Unilateral neglect, representational schema, and consciousness. *Brain, 102,* 609–618.

Bizzi, E., & Mussa-Ivaldi, F.A. (1990). Muscle properties and the control of arm movement. In D. Osherson, S.M. Kosslyn, & J.M. Hollerbach (Eds.), *An invitation to cognitive science Vol. 2: Visual cognition and action,* pp.213–242. Cambridge, MA.: MIT Press.

Bjork, R.A., & Whitten, W.B. (1974). Recency sensitive retrieval processes. *Cognitive Psychology, 6,* 173–189.

Brandimonte, M., & Gerbino, W. (1993). Mental image reversal and verbal recoding: When ducks become rabbits. *Memory & Cognition, 21,* 23–33.

Brandimonte, M., Hitch, G.J., & Bishop, D. (1992a). Influence of short-term memory codes on visual image processing: Evidence from image transformation tasks. *Journal of Experimental Psychology: Learning, Memory, and Cognition, 18*, 157–165.

Brandimonte, M., Hitch, G.J., & Bishop, D. (1992b). Verbal recoding of visual stimuli impairs mental image transformations. *Memory and Cognition, 20*, 449–455.

Broadbent, D.E., & Broadbent, M.H.P. (1981). Recency effects in visual memory. *Quarterly Journal of Experimental Psychology, 33*A, 1–15.

Brooks, L.R. (1967). The suppression of visualisation by reading. *Quarterly Journal of Experimental Psychology, 19*, 289–299.

Brooks, L.R. (1968). Spatial and verbal components in the act of recall. *Canadian Journal of Psychology, 22*, 349–368.

Brown, G.D.A. (1989). A connectionist model of phonological short-term memory. In *Proceedings of the eleventh annual conference of the Cognitive Science Society*. Hillsdale, NJ: Lawrence Erlbaum Associates Inc.

Brown, G.D.A. (1990). A neural net model of human short-term memory development. In *Proceedings of the EURASIP workshop on neural networks*. Heidelberg: Springer-Verlag.

Burgess, N., & Hitch, G.J. (1992). Toward a network model of the articulatory loop. *Journal of Memory and Language, 31*, 429–460.

Butters, N., Barton, M., & Brody, B.A. (1970). Role of the parietal lobe in the mediation of cross modal associations and reversible operations in space. *Cortex, 6*, 174–190.

Butters, N., & Cermack, L.S. (1986). A case study of the forgetting of autobiographical knowledge: Implications for the study of retrograde amnesia. In D.C. Rubin (Ed.), *Autobiographical memory*, pp.253–289. Cambridge, MA: Cambridge University Press.

Campbell, J.I.D., & Graham, D.J. (1985). Mental multiplication skill: structure, process, and acquisition. *Canadian Journal of Psychology, 39*, 338–366.

Cantone, G., Orsini, A., Grossi, D., & De Michele, G. (1978). Verbal and spatial memory span in dementia. *Acta Neurologica Napoli, 33*, 175–183.

Capitani, E., Della Sala, S., Logie, R., & Spinnler, H. (1992). Recency, primacy and memory: Reappraising and standardising the serial position curve. *Cortex, 28*, 315–342.

Caplan, D., & Waters, G.S. (1990). Short-term memory and language comprehension: A critical review of the neuropsychological literature. In G. Vallar & T. Shallice (Eds.), *Neuropsychological impairments of short-term memory*, pp. 337–389. Cambridge: Cambridge University Press.

Caramazza, A. (1986). On drawing inferences about the structure of the normal cognitive system from the analysis of patterns in impaired performances: The case for single-case study. *Brain and Cognition, 5*, 41–66.

Caramazza, A., & Hillis, A.E. (1990). Levels of representation, co-ordinate frames, and unilateral neglect. *Cognitive Neuropsychology, 7*, 1073–1078.

Caramazza, A., & McCloskey, M. (1988). The case for single-patient studies. *Cognitive Neuropsychology, 5*, 517–527.

Case, R.D., Kurland, D.M., & Goldberg, J. (1982). Operational efficiency and the growth of short-term memory span. *Journal of Experimental Child Psychology, 33*, 386–404.

Cave, K.R., & Kosslyn, S.M. (1989). Varieties of size-specific visual selection. *Journal of Experimental Psychology: General, 118*, 148–164.

Cech, C.G. (1989). Congruity and the expectancy hypothesis. *Journal of Experimental Psychology: Learning, Memory, and Cognition, 15,* 1129–1133.

Chambers, D., & Reisberg, D. (1985). Can mental images be ambiguous? *Journal of Experimental Psychology: Human Perception and Performance, 11,* 317–328.

Clark, H.H. (1969). Linguistic processes in deductive reasoning. *Psychological Review, 76*, 387–404.

Conrad, R. (1964). Acoustic confusions in immediate memory. *British Journal of Psychology, 55*, 75–84.

Cooper, L.A. (1975). Mental rotation of random two-dimensional shapes. *Cognitive Psychology, 7*, 20–43.

Cooper, L.A. (1976). Demonstration of a mental analog of an external rotation. *Perception and Psychophysics, 19*, 296–302.

Cooper, L.A. (1991). Dissociable aspects of the mental representation of visual objects. In R.H. Logie & M. Denis (Eds.), *Mental images in human cognition.* Amsterdam: Elsevier.

Cooper, L.A., & Podgorny, P. (1976). Mental transformations and visual comparison processes: Effects of complexity and similarity. *Journal of Experimental Psychology: Human Perception and Performance, 2*, 503–514.

Cooper, L.A., & Shepard, R.N. (1973). Chronometric studies of the rotation of mental images. In W.G. Chase (Ed.), *Visual information processing* (pp. 75–176). New York: Academic Press.

Corballis, M.C. (1986). Is mental rotation controlled or automatic? *Memory and Cognition, 14*, 124–128

Corkin, S. (1965). Tactually guided maze learning in man: Effects of unilateral cortical excisions and bilateral cortical lesions. *Neuropsychologia, 3*, 339–351.

Cornoldi, C., Cortesi, A., & Preti, D. (1991). Individual differences in the capacity limitations of visuospatial short-term memory: Research on sighted and totally congenitally blind people. *Memory & Cognition, 19* (5), 459–468.

Cornoldi, C., Logie, R.H., Brandimonte, M., Kaufmann, G., & Reisberg, D. (in press). *Perception and mental representation.* New York: Oxford University Press.

Cowan, N. (1988). Evolving conceptions of memory storage, selective attention, and their mutual constraints within the human information-processing system. *Psychological Bulletin, 104*, 163–191.

Cowan, N. (1993). Activation, attention, and short-term memory. *Memory and Cognition, 21*, 162–167.

Craik, F.I.M., & Lockhart, R.S. (1972). Levels of processing: A framework for memory research. *Journal of Verbal Learning and Verbal Behavior, 11*, 671–684.

Craik, F.I.M., & Tulving, E. (1975). Depth of processing and the retention of words in episodic memory. *Journal of Experimental Psychology: General, 104,* 268–294.

Crowder, R.G. (1976). *Principles of learning and memory.* Hillsdale, NJ: Lawrence Erlbaum Associates Inc.

Curtis, D.W., Paulos, M.A., & Rule, S.J. (1973). Relation between disjunctive reaction time and stimulus difference. *Journal of Experimental Psychology, 99,* 167–173.

Damasio, A.R., & Benton, A.L. (1979). Impairment of hand movements under visual guidance. *Neurology, 29,* 170–174.

Damasio, A.R., Graff-Radford, N.R., Eslinger, P.J., Damasio, H., & Kassell, N. (1985). Amnesia following basal forebrain lesions. *Archives of Neurology, 42,* 263–271.

Daneman, M., & Carpenter, P.A. (1980). Individual differences in working memory and reading. *Journal of Verbal Learning and Verbal Behavior, 19,* 450–466.

Daneman, M., & Carpenter, P.A. (1983). Individual differences in integrating information between and within sentences. *Journal of Experimental Psychology: Learning Memory and Cognition, 9,* 561–584.

Dehaene, S. (1992). Varieties of numerical abilities. *Cognition, 44,* 1–42.

Della Sala, S., & Logie, R.H. (1993). When working memory does not work: The role of working memory in neuropsychology. In F. Boller & H. Spinnler (Eds.), *Handbook of neuropsychology, Vol. 8,* pp.1–63. Amsterdam: Elsevier Publishers BV.

Della Sala, S., Logie, R.H., Marchetti, C., & Wynn, V. (1991). Case studies in working memory: A case for single cases? *Cortex, 27,* 169–191.

Della Sala, S., Pasetti, C., & Sempio, P. (1987). Deficit of the "Primary Effect" in Parkinsonians interpreted by means of the working memory model. *Swiss Archives of Neurology, Neurosurgery and Psychiatry, 138,* 5–14.

Della Sala, S., & Spinnler, H. (1986). "Indifférence Amnésique" in a case of global amnesia following acute brain hypoxia. *European Neurology, 25,* 98–109.

Denis, M. (1989). *Image et Cognition.* Paris: Presses Universitaires de France.

Denis, M., & Cocude, M. (1989). Scanning visual images generated from verbal descriptions. *European Journal of Cognitive Psychology, 1,* 293–307.

De Renzi, E. (1982). *Disorders of space exploration and cognition.* Chichester: Wiley.

De Renzi, E., Faglioni, P., & Previdi, P. (1977). Spatial memory and hemispheric locus of lesion. *Cortex, 13,* 424–433.

De Renzi, E., & Nichelli, P. (1975). Verbal and nonverbal short term memory impairment following hemispheric damage. *Cortex, 11,* 341–353.

Derrington, A.M., & Lennie, P. (1984). Spatial and temporal contrast sensitivities of neurones in lateral geniculate nucleus of macaque. *Journal of Physiology, 357,* 219–240.

De Yoe, E.A., & Van Essen, D.C. (1988). Concurrent processing streams in monkey visual cortex. *Trends in Neuroscience, 11,* 219–226,.

Eddy, J.K., & Glass, A.L. (1981). Reading and listening to high and low imagery sentences. *Journal of Verbal Learning and Verbal Behavior, 20,* 333–345.

Ellis, N.C. (1991). Word meaning and the links between the verbal system and modalities of perception and imagery. In R.H. Logie & M. Denis (Eds.), *Mental images in human cognition,* pp.313–329. Amsterdam: North Holland Press.

Ellis, N.C., & Hennelley, R.A. (1980). A bilingual word length effect: Implications for intelligence testing and the relative ease of mental calculation in Welsh and English. *British Journal of Psychology, 71,* 43–52.

Engelkamp, J. (1991) Imagery and enactment in paired-associate learning. In R.H. Logie & M. Denis (Eds.), *Mental images in human cognition*. Amsterdam: North Holland Press.

Engelkamp, J., Zimmer, H.D., & Denis, M. (1989). Paired associate learning of action verbs with visual- or motor-imaginal encoding instructions. *Psychological Research, 50*, 257–263.

Epstein, M.L. (1980). The relationship of mental imagery and mental rehearsal to performance on a motor task. *Journal of Sport Psychology, 2*, 211–220.

Evans, F.J. (1978). Monitoring attention deployment by random number generation: An index to measure subjective randomness. *Bulletin of the Psychonomic Society, 12*, 35–38.

Eysenck, M.W., & Keane, M.T. (1990). *Cognitive psychology: A student's handbook*. Hove, UK: Lawrence Erlbaum Associates Ltd.

Fabiani, M., Buckley, J., Gratton, G., Coles, M., Donchin, E., & Logie, R.H. (1989). The training of complex task performance. *Acta Psychologica, 71*, 259–299.

Farah, M.J. (1984). The neurological basis of mental imagery: A componential analysis. *Cognition, 18*, 245–272.

Farah, M.J. (1988). Is visual imagery really visual? Overlooked evidence from neuropsychology. *Psychological Review, 95*, 307–317.

Farah, M.J., Hammond, K.M., Levine, D.N., & Calvanio, R. (1988). Visual and spatial mental imagery: Dissociable systems of representation. *Cognitive Psychology, 20*, 439–462.

Farmer, E.W., Berman, J.V.F., & Fletcher, Y.L. (1986). Evidence for a visuo-spatial scratch-pad in working memory. *Quarterly Journal of Experimental Psychology, 38A*, 675–688.

Finke, R. (1989). *Principles of mental imagery*. Cambridge, MA: MIT Press.

Finke, R., & Pinker, S. (1982). Spontaneous imagery scanning in mental extrapolation. *Journal of Experimental Psychology: Learning, Memory and Cognition, 8*, 142–147.

Finke, R., Pinker, S., & Farah, M.J. (1989). Reinterpreting visual patterns in mental imagery. *Cognitive Science, 13*, 51–78.

Finke, R., & Slayton, K. (1988). Explorations of creative visual synthesis in mental imagery. *Memory and Cognition, 16*, 252–257.

Frick, R.W. (1987). A dissociation of conscious visual imagery and visual short-term memory. *Neuropsychologia, 25*, 707–712.

Frick, R.W. (1988). Issues of representation and limited capacity in the visuo-spatial sketchpad. *British Journal of Psychology, 79*, 289–308.

Fuchs, A., Goschke, T., & Gude, D. (1988). On the role of imagery in linear syllogistic reasoning. *Psychological Research, 50*, 43–49.

Gathercole, S., & Baddeley, A.D. (1989). Evaluation of the role of phonological STM in the development of vocabulary in children: A longitudinal study. *Journal of Memory and Language, 28*, 200–213.

Gathercole, S., & Baddeley, A.D. (1990). The role of phonological memory in vocabulary acquisition: A study of young children learning arbitrary names of toys. *British Journal of Psychology, 81*, 439–454.

Georgopoloulos, A.P., Kalaska, J.F., Caminiti, R., & Massey, J.T. (1982). On the relations between the direction of two-dimensional arm movements and cell discharge in primate motor cortex. *Journal of Neuroscience, 2*, 1527–1537.

Georgopoloulos, A.P., Kalaska, J.F., Caminiti, R., & Massey, J.T. (1983). Spatial coding of movement: A hypothesis concerning the coding of movement direction by motor cortical populations. In J. Massion, J. Paillard, W. Schultz, & M. Wiesendanger (Eds.), *Neural coding of motor performance. Experimental Brain Research Supplement, 7,* 327–336.

Gilhooly, K.J., Logie, R.H., Wetherick, N.E., & Wynn, V. (1993). Working memory and strategies in syllogistic reasoning tasks. *Memory and Cognition, 21,* 115–124.

Glanzer, M., & Cunitz, A.R. (1966). Two storage mechanisms in free recall. *Journal of Verbal Learning and Verbal Behavior, 5,* 351–360.

Glass, A.L., Eddy, J.K., & Schwanenflugel, J. (1980). The verification of high and low-imagery sentences. *Journal of Experimental Psychology: Human Learning and Memory, 6,* 692–704.

Glenberg, A.M., Bradley, M.M., Stevenson, J.A., Kraus, T.A., Tkachuk, M.J., Gretz, A.L., Fish, J.H., & Turpin, B.A.M. (1980). A two-process account of long-term serial position effects. *Journal of Experimental Psychology: Human Learning and Memory, 6,* 355–369.

Goldenberg, G., Podreka, I., Steiner, M., Franzen, P., & Deecke, L. (1991). Contributions of occipital and temporal brain regions to visual and acoustic imagery—a SPECT study. *Neuropsychologia, 29,* 695–701.

Gopher, D., Weil, M., & Siegel, D. (1989). Practice under changing priorities: An approach to the training of complex skills. *Acta Psychologica, 71,* 147–177.

Greene, R.L. (1986). Sources of recency effects in free recall. *Psychological Bulletin, 99,* 221–228.

Grossberg, S., & Stone, G. (1986). Neural dynamics of attention switching and temporal order information in short-term memory. *Memory and Cognition, 14,* 451–468.

Halligan, P.W., & Marshall, J.C. (1991). Left neglect for near but not far space in man. *Nature, 350,* 498–500.

Halligan, P.W., & Marshall, J.C. (1992). Left visuo-spatial neglect: A meaningless entity? *Cortex, 28,* 525–535.

Hanley, J.R., Pearson, N.A., & Young, A.W. (1990). Impaired memory for new visual forms. *Brain, 113,* 1131–1148.

Hanley, J.R., Young, A.W., & Pearson, N.A. (1991). Impairment of the visuo-spatial sketch pad. *Quarterly Journal of Experimental Psychology, 43A,* 101–125.

Hasher, L., & Zacks, R T. (1988). Working memory, comprehension and aging: A review and a new view. *The Psychology of Learning & Motivation, 22,* 193–225.

Hayes, J.R. (1973). On the function of visual imagery in elementary mathematics. In W.G. Chase (Ed.), *Visual information processing,* pp.177–214. New York: Academic Press.

Hayes, N.A., & Broadbent, D.E. (1988). Two modes of learning for interactive tasks. *Cognition, 28,* 249–276.

Henderson, J.M., & Well, A.D. (1985). Symbolic comparisons with and without perceptual referents: Is interval information used? *Memory and Cognition, 13,* 176–182.

Hinton, G.E., McClelland, J.L., & Rumelhart, D.E. (1986). Distributed representations. In D.E. Rumelhart & J.L McClelland (Eds.), *Parallel distributed processing: Explorations in the microstructure of cognition. Volume 1: Foundations* (pp.77–109). Cambridge, MA: MIT Press.

Hinton, G.E., & Plaut, D.C. (1987). Using fast weights to deblur old memories. *Proceedings of the ninth annual conference of the Cognitive Science Society,* pp. 177–186. Hillsdale, NJ: Lawrence Erlbaum Associates Inc.

Hitch, G.J., & Baddeley, A.D. (1976). Verbal reasoning and working memory. *Quarterly Journal of Experimental Psychology, 28,* 603–621.

Hitch, G.J., & Halliday, M.S. (1983). Working memory in children. *Philosophical Transactions of the Royal Society of London B, 302,* 325–340.

Hitch, G.J., Halliday, M.S., Schaafstal, A.M., & Schraagen, J.M.C. (1988). Visual working memory in young children. *Memory and Cognition, 16,* 120–132.

Hitch, G.J., & Walker, P. (1991). *Visuo-spatial working memory in children and in adults.* Paper presented at the International Conference on Memory, University of Lancaster, United Kingdom.

Hitch, G.J., Woodin, M.E., & Baker, S. (1989). Visual and phonological components of working memory in children. *Memory and Cognition, 17,* 175–185.

Hollerbach, J.M. (1990). Planning of arm movements. In D. Osherson, S.M. Kosslyn, & J.M. Hollerbach (Eds.), *An invitation to cognitive science Vol. 2: Visual cognition and action,* pp.183–211. Cambridge, MA: MIT Press.

Holyoak, K., & Walker, J.H. (1976). Subjective magnitude information in semantic orderings. *Journal of Verbal Learning and Verbal Behavior, 15,* 287–299.

Hoosain, R., & Salili, F. (1988). Language differences, working memory and mathematical ability. In M.M. Gruneberg, P.E. Morris, & R.N. Sykes (Eds.), *Practical aspects of memory: Current research and issues,* Vol. 2, pp.512–517. London: Wiley & Sons.

Houghton, G. (1990). The problem of serial order: A neural network model of sequence learning and recall. In R. Dale, C. Mellish, & M. Zock (Eds.), *Current research in natural language generation,* pp. 287–319. London: Academic Press.

Hue, C., & Ericsson, J.R. (1988). Short-term memory for Chinese characters and radicals. *Memory and Cognition, 16,* 196–205.

Hulme, C., Maughan, S., & Brown, G.D.A. (1991). Memory for familiar and unfamiliar words: Evidence for a long-term memory contribution to short-term memory span. *Journal of Memory and Language, 30,* 685–701.

Hulme, C., Thomson, N., Muir, C., & Lawrence, A. (1984). Speech rate and the development of short-term memory span. *Journal of Experimental Child Psychology, 38,* 241–153.

Hyde, T.S., & Jenkins, J.J. (1973). Recall for words as a function of semantic, graphic, and syntactic orienting tasks. *Journal of Verbal Learning and Verbal Behavior, 12,* 471–480.

Jakobson, L.S., Archibald, Y.M., Carey, D.P., & Goodale, M.A. (1991). A kinematic analysis of reaching and grasping movements in a patient recovering from optic ataxia. *Neuropsychologia, 29,* 803–809.

James, W. (1890). *Principles of Psychology, Vol. 1.* (1905 ed.). London: Methuen & Co.

Jeannerod, M. (1986). The formation of finger grip during prehension: A cortically mediated visuomotor pattern. *Behavioural Brain Research, 19,* 99–116.

Johnson, P. (1982). The functional equivalence of imagery and movement. *Quarterly Journal of Experimental Psychology, 34A,* 349–365.

Johnson-Laird, P.N. (1983). *Mental models*. Cambridge: Cambridge University Press.

Jones, G.V. (1985). Deep dyslexia, imageability and ease of predication. *Brain and Language, 24,* 1–19.

Jones, G.V. (1988). Imageability and a performance measure of predicability. In M. Denis, J. Engelkamp, & J.T.E. Richardson (Eds.), *Cognitive and neuropsychological approaches to mental imagery*. Amsterdam: Martinus Nijhoff, BV.

Jordan, M.I. (1986). Attractor dynamics and parallelism in a connectionist sequential machine. *Proceedings of the eighth annual conference of the Cognitive Science Society*. Hillsdale, NJ: Lawrence Erlbaum Associates Inc.

Just, M., & Carpenter, P. (1992). A capacity theory of comprehension: Individual differences in working memory. *Psychological Review, 99,* 122–149.

Kaufmann, G., & Helstrup, T. (1993). Mental imagery: Fixed or multiple meanings? In B. Roskos-Ewoldsen, M.J. Intons-Peterson, & R.E. Anderson (Eds.), *Imagery, creativity, and discovery: A cognitive perspective*. Amsterdam: North Holland Press.

Kerr, N. (1983). The role of vision in visual imagery experiments: Evidence from the congenitally blind. *Journal of Experimental Psychology: General, 112,* 265–277.

Kerst, S.M., & Howard, J.H. (1977). Mental comparisons for ordered information on abstract and concrete dimensions. *Memory and Cognition, 5,* 227–234.

Kikuchi, T. (1987). Temporal characteristics of visual memory. *Journal of Experimental Psychology: Human Perception and Performance, 13,* 464–477.

Kimura, D. (1963). Right temporal-lobe damage. *Archives of Neurology, 8,* 264–271.

Kinsbourne, M. (1977). Hemi-neglect and hemisphere rivalry. In E.A. Weinstein & R.P. Friedland (Eds.), *Advances in neurology*, Vol. 18, pp.41–49. New York: Raven Press.

Kinsbourne, M. (1993). Orientational bias model of unilateral neglect: Evidence from attentional gradients within hemispace. In I.H. Robertson & J.C. Marshall (Eds.), *Unilateral neglect: Clinical and experimental studies*. Hove, UK: Lawrence Erlbaum Associates Ltd.

Kosslyn, S.M. (1980). *Image and mind*. Cambridge, MA: Harvard University Press.

Kosslyn, S.M. (1987). Seeing and imagining in the cerebral hemispheres: A computational approach. *Psychological Review, 94,* 148–175.

Kosslyn, S.M. (1991). A cognitive neuroscience of visual cognition: Further developments. In R.H. Logie & M. Denis (Eds.), *Mental images in human cognition*, pp.352–381. Amsterdam: Elsevier.

Kosslyn, S.M., Ball, T.M., & Reiser, B.J. (1978). Visual images preserve metric spatial information: Evidence from studies of image scanning. *Journal of Experimental Psychology: Human Perception and Performance, 4,* 47–60.

Kosslyn, S.M. Cave, C.B., Provost, D.A., & von Gierke, S.M. (1988). Sequential processes in image generation. *Cognitive Psychology, 20,* 319–343.

Kosslyn, S.M., Chabris, C.F., Marsolek, C.J., & Koenig, O. (1992). Categorical versus coordinate spatial relations: Computational analyses and computer simulations. *Journal of Experimental Psychology: Human Perception and Performance, 18,* 562–577.

Kosslyn, S.M., Flynn, R.A., Amsterdam, J.B., & Wang, G. (1990). Components of high-level vision: A cognitive neuroscience analysis and accounts of neurological syndromes. *Cognition, 34,* 203–277.

La Pointe, L.B., & Engle, R.W. (1990). Simple and complex word spans as measures of working memory capacity. *Journal of Experimental Psychology: Learning, Memory, and Cognition, 16,* 1118–1133.

Larsen, A., & Bundesen, C. (1978). Size scaling in visual pattern recognition. *Journal of Experimental Psychology: Human Perception and Performance, 4,* 1–20.

Levy, B.A. (1971). The role of articulation in auditory and visual short-term memory. *Journal of Verbal Learning and Verbal Behavior, 10,* 123–132.

Levy, B.A. (1975). Vocalization and suppression effects in sentence memory. *Journal of Verbal Learning and Verbal Behavior, 14,* 304–316.

Locke, J. (1690). *An essay concerning human understanding.* London (1st ed.).

Logie, R.H. (1986). Visuo-spatial processing in working memory. *Quarterly Journal of Experimental Psychology, 38A,* 229–247.

Logie, R.H. (1989). Characteristics of visual short-term memory. *European Journal of Cognitive Psychology, 1,* 275–284.

Logie, R.H. (1991). Visuo-spatial short-term memory: Visual working memory or visual buffer? In C. Cornoldi & M. McDaniel (Eds.), *Imagery and cognition,* pp.77–102. Berlin: Springer-Verlag.

Logie, R.H. (1993). Working memory in everyday cognition. In G.M. Davies & R.H. Logie (Eds.), *Memory in everyday life,* pp. 173–218. Amsterdam: Elsevier Publishers B.V.

Logie, R.H. (in press). The seven ages of working memory. In J.T.E. Richardson (Ed.), *Counterpoints: Working memory in human cognition.* New York: Oxford University Press.

Logie, R.H., & Baddeley, A.D. (1987). Cognitive processes in counting. *Journal of Experimental Psychology: Learning, Memory and Cognition, 13 ,* 310–326.

Logie, R.H., Baddeley, A.D., Mane, A., Donchin, E., & Sheptak, R. (1989). Working memory and the analysis of a complex skill by secondary task methodology. *Acta Psychologica, 71,* 53–87.

Logie, R.H., Della Sala, S., Laiacona, M., Chalmers, P., & Wynn, V. (1993). *Group effects, individual differences, and cognitive neuropsychology: The case of verbal short-term memory.* Paper submitted for publication.

Logie, R.H., Gilhooly, K.J., & Wynn, V. (1994). Counting on working memory in arithmetic problem solving. *Memory and Cognition, 22,* 395–410.

Logie, R.H., & Marchetti, C. (1991). Visuo-spatial working memory: Visual, spatial or central executive? In R.H. Logie & M. Denis (Eds.), *Mental images in human cognition,* pp.105–115. Amsterdam: North Holland Press

Logie, R.H., & Salway, A.F.S. (1990). Working memory and modes of thinking: A secondary task approach. In K. Gilhooly, M. Keane, R. Logie, & G. Erdos (Eds.), *Lines of thinking: Reflections on the psychology of thought, Vol. 2.* pp.99–113. Chichester: Wiley.

Logie, R.H., Trivelli, C., & Della Sala, S. (1993, September). *Phonological short-term memory is not the locus of recency in verbal free recall.* Paper presented to the annual conference of the British Psychological Society Cognitive Psychology Section, Cambridge.

Logie, R.H., Zucco, G., & Baddeley, A.D. (1990). Interference with visual short-term memory. *Acta Psychologica, 75*, 55–74.

Longoni, A.M., Richardson, J.T.E., & Aiello, A. (1993). Articulatory rehearsal and phonological storage in working memory. *Memory and Cognition, 21*, 11–22.

Luria, A.R. (1966). *Higher cortical functions in man*. London: Tavistock.

Luria, A.R., Sokolov, E.N., & Kilmkowski, M. (1967). Towards a neurodynamic analysis of memory disturbances with lesions of the left temporal lobe. *Neuropsychologia, 5*, 1–11.

Mandler, J. M., & Johnson, N. (1976). Some of the thousand words a picture is worth. *Journal of Experimental Psychology: Human Learning and Memory, 2*, 529–540.

Marr, D. (1982). *Vision*. San Francisco: Freeman.

Marschark, M. (1985). Imagery and organization in the recall of prose. *Journal of Memory and Language, 24*, 734–745.

Marschark, M., & Cornoldi, C. (1991). Imagery and verbal memory. In C. Cornoldi & M.A. McDaniel (Eds.), *Imagery and cognition*, pp.133–182. New York: Springer-Verlag.

Marschark, M., & Hunt, R.R. (1989). A reexamination of the role of imagery in learning and memory. *Journal of Experimental Psychology: Learning, Memory, and Cognition, 15*, 710–720.

Marschark, M., & Paivio, A. (1977). Integrative processing of concrete and abstract sentences. *Journal of Verbal Learning and Verbal Behavior, 16*, 217–231.

Marschark, M., & Surian, L. (1989). Why does imagery improve memory? *European Journal of Cognitive Psychology, 1*, 251–263.

Marschark, M., Warner, J., Thomson, R., & Huffman, C. (1991). Concreteness, imagery and memory for prose. In R.H. Logie & M. Denis (Eds.), *Mental images in human cognition*, pp.193–207. Amsterdam: Elsevier.

Marteniuk, R.G. (1976). Cognitive information processes in motor short-term memory and movement production. In G. Stelmach (Ed.), *Motor control: Issues and trends*. New York: Academic Press.

Martin, M. (1978). Memory span as a measure of individual differences in memory capacity. *Memory and Cognition, 6*, 194–198.

Martin, R.C. (1987). Articulatory and phonological deficits in short-term memory and their relation to syntactic processing. *Brain and Language, 32*, 159–192.

Matthews, W.A. (1983). The effects of concurrent secondary tasks on the use of imagery in a free recall task. *Acta Psychologica, 53*, 231–241.

Maunsell, J.H.R., & Newsome, W.T. (1987). Visual processing in monkey extrastriate cortex. *Annual Review of Neuroscience, 10*, 363–401.

McCarthy, R.A., & Warrington, E.K. (1987). Understanding: A function of short-term memory? *Brain, 110*, 1565–1578.

McCarthy, R.A., & Warrington, E.K. (1990a). *Cognitive neuropsychology: A clinical introduction*. London: Academic Press.

McCarthy, R.A., & Warrington, E.K. (1990b). Auditory-verbal span of apprehension: A phenomenon in search of a function? In G. Vallar & T. Shallice (Eds.), *Neuropsychological impairments of short-term memory*, pp.167–186. Cambridge, UK: Cambridge University Press.

McClelland, J.L., & Rumelhart, D.E. (1986). *Parallel distributed processing: Explorations in the microstructure of cognition. Vol. 2: Psychological and biological models.* Cambridge, MA: MIT Press.

McCloskey, M. (1992). Cognitive mechanisms in numerical processing: Evidence from acquired dyscalculia. *Cognition, 44,* 107–157.

McDaniel, M.A., & Pressley, M. (Eds.) (1987). *Imagery and related mnemonic processes: Theories, individual differences, and applications.* New York: Springer-Verlag.

McGlinchey-Berroth, R., Milberg, W.P., Verfaellie, M., Alexander, M., & Kilduff, P.T. (1993). Semantic processing in the neglected visual field: Evidence from a lexical decision task. *Cognitive Neuropsychology, 10,* 79–108.

Millar, S. (1990). Imagery and blindness. In P.J. Hampson, D.F. Marks, & J.T.E. Richardson (Eds.), *Imagery: Current developments.* London: Routledge.

Milner, B. (1965). Visually guided maze learning in man: Effect of bilateral hippocampal, bilateral frontal and unilateral cerebral lesions. *Neuropsychologia, 3,* 317–338.

Milner, B. (1968). Visual recognition and recall after right temporal-lobe excision in man. *Neuropsychologia, 6,* 191–209.

Milner, B. (1971). Interhemispheric differences and psychological processes. *British Medical Bulletin, 27,* 272–277.

Milner, B., Corkin, S., & Teuber, H-L. (1968). Further analysis of the hippocampal amnesic syndrome: Fourteen year follow-up study of H.M. *Neuropsychologia, 6,* 215–234.

Mishkin, M., Ungerleider, L.G., & Macko, K.A. (1983). Object vision and spatial vision: Two cortical pathways. *Trends in Neuroscience, 6,* 414–417.

Mitchell, D.B., & Richman, C.L. (1980). Confirmed reservation: Mental travel. *Journal of Experimental Psychology: Human Perception and Performance, 6,* 58–66.

Mohr, G., & Engelkamp, J. (1991). Size comparison and pictorial material. In R.H. Logie & M. Denis (Eds.), *Mental images in human cognition.* Amsterdam: North Holland Press.

Monsell, S. (1987). On the relation between lexical input and output pathways for speech. In A. Allport, D. MacKay, W. Prinz, & E. Sheerer (Eds.), *Language perception and production.* London: Academic Press.

Morris, N. (1987). Exploring the visuo-spatial scratch pad. *Quarterly Journal of Experimental Psychology, 39*A, 409–430.

Morris, R.G., & Baddeley, A.D. (1988). Primary and working memory functioning in Alzheimer-type dementia. *Journal of Clinical and Experimental Neuropsychology, 10,* 279–296.

Moyer, R.S. (1973). Comparing objects in memory: Evidence suggesting an internal psychophysics. *Perception and Psychophysics, 13,* 180–184.

Moyer, R.S., & Bayer R.H. (1976). Mental comparison and the symbolic distance effect. *Cognitive Psychology, 8,* 228–246.

Murray, D. (1965). Vocalization-at-presentation, with varying presentation rates. *Quarterly Journal of Experimental Psychology, 17,* 47–56.

Murray, D. (1968). Articulation and acoustic confusability in short-term memory. *Journal of Experimental Psychology, 78,* 679–684.

Mussa-Ivaldi, F.A. (1988). Do neurons in the motor cortex encode movement direction? An alternative hypothesis. *Neuroscience Letters, 91,* 106–111.

Naveh-Benjamin, M., & Ayres, T.J. (1986). Digit span, reading rate, and linguistic relativity. *Quarterly Journal of Experimental Psychology*, *38*, 739–751.

Nipher, F.E. (1876). On the distribution of errors in numbers written from memory. *Transactions of the Academy of Science of St. Louis*, *3*, CCX–CCXI.

Norman, D.A. (1968). Toward a theory of memory and attention. *Psychological Review*, *75*, 522–536.

Norris, D. (1990). Dynamic net model of human speech recognition. In G.T. Altmann (Ed.), *Cognitive models of speech processing: Psycholinguistic and computational perspectives*. Cambridge, MA: MIT Press.

Paivio, A. (1971). *Imagery and verbal processes*. New York: Holt, Rinehart & Winston.

Paivio, A. (1975). Perceptual comparisons through the mind's eye. *Memory and Cognition*, *3*, 635–647.

Paivio, A. (1978). Comparisons of mental clocks. *Journal of Experimental Psychology: Human Perception and Performance*, *4*, 61–71.

Paivio, A. (1986). *Mental representations: A dual coding approach*. New York, Oxford University Press.

Paivio, A. (1991). *Images in mind: The evolution of a theory*. Hemel Hempstead: Harvester Wheatsheaf.

Paivio, A., & Csapo, K. (1969). Concrete image and verbal memory codes. *Journal of Experimental Psychology*, *80*, 279–285.

Perani, D., Bressi, S., Cappa, S.F., Vallar, G., Alberoni, M., Grassi, F., Caltagirone, C., Cipolotti, L., Franceschi, M., Lenzi, G.L., & Fazio, F. (1993). Evidence of multiple memory systems in the human brain. *Brain*, *116*, 903–919.

Perenin, M.-T., & Vighetto, A. (1988). Optic ataxia: A specific disruption in visuomotor mechanisms. *Brain*, *111*, 643–674.

Perfetti, C.A., & Goldman, S.R. (1976). Discourse memory and reading comprehension skill. *Journal of Verbal Learning and Verbal Behavior*, *14*, 33–42.

Petrides, M. (1985). Deficits on conditional associative learning tasks after frontal and temporal lobe lesions in man. *Neuropsychologia*, *23*, 601–614.

Phillips, W.A. (1983). Short-term visual memory. *Philosophical Transactions of the Royal Society of London*, *B302*, 295–309.

Phillips, W.A., & Christie, D.F.M. (1977a). Components of visual memory. *Quarterly Journal of Experimental Psychology*, *29*, 117–133.

Phillips, W.A., & Christie, D.F.M. (1977b). Interference with visualization. *Quarterly Journal of Experimental Psychology*, *29*, 637–650.

Pigott, S., & Milner, B. (1993). Memory for different aspects of complex visual scenes after unilateral temporal or frontal lobe resection. *Neuropsychologia*, *31*, 1–15.

Pinker, S. (1988). A computational theory of the mental imagery medium. In M. Denis, J. Engelkamp, & J.T.E. Richardson (Eds.), *Cognitive and neuropsychological approaches to mental imagery*, pp.17–32. Amsterdam: Martinus Nijhoff, BV.

Podgorny, P., & Shepard, R.N. (1978). Functional representations common to visual perception and imagination. *Journal of Experimental Psychology: Human Perception and Performance*, *9*, 21–35.

Posner, M. (1967). Characteristics of visual and kinaesthetic memory codes. *Journal of Experimental Psychology*, *75*, 103–107.

Posner, M., Cohen, Y., & Rafal, R.D. (1982). Neural systems control of spatial orienting. *Philosophical Transactions of the Royal Society of London, Series B, 298*, 187–198.

Postman, L. (1975). Verbal learning and memory. *Annual Review of Psychology 26*, 291–335.

Potts, G.R. (1972). Information processing strategies used in the encoding of linear orderings. *Journal of Verbal Learning and Verbal Behavior, 11*, 727–740.

Potts, G.R. (1974). Storing and retrieving information about ordered relationships. *Journal of Experimental Psychology, 103*, 431–439.

Purdy, J.E., & Olmstead, K.M. (1984). New estimate for storage time in sensory memory. *Perceptual and Motor Skills 59*(3), 683–686.

Pylyshyn, Z.W. (1973). What the mind's eye tells the mind's brain: A critique of mental imagery. *Psychological Bulletin, 80*, 1–24.

Pylyshyn, Z.W. (1981). The imagery debate: Analogue media versus tacit knowledge. *Psychological Review, 88*, 16–45.

Pylyshyn, Z.W. (1984). *Computation and cognition*. Cambridge, MA: MIT Press.

Quinn, J.G. (1988). Interference effects in the visuo-spatial sketchpad. In M. Denis, J. Engelkamp, & J.T.E. Richardson (Eds.), *Cognitive and neuropsychological approaches to mental imagery*, pp.181–189. Dordrecht: Martinus Nijhoff.

Quinn, J.G. (1991). Encoding and maintenance of information in visual working memory. In R.H. Logie & M. Denis (Eds.), *Mental images in human cognition*, pp.105–115. Amsterdam: Elsevier.

Quinn, J.G. (1994). Towards a clarification of spatial processing. *Quarterly Journal of Experimental Psychology, 47A*, 465–480.

Quinn, J.G., & McConnell, J. (1994). *The irrelevant picture effect in the visuo-spatial sketchpad*. Paper presented at the International Conference on Working Memory, Cambridge, UK.

Quinn, J.G., & Ralston, G.E. (1986). Movement and attention in visual working memory. *The Quarterly Journal of Experimental Psychology, 38A*, 689–703.

Ratcliff, G. (1979). Spatial thought, mental rotation and the right cerebral hemisphere. *Neuropsychologia, 17*, 48–54.

Reisberg, D. (in press). The non-ambiguity of mental images. In C. Cornoldi, R.H. Logie, M. Brandimonte, G. Kaufmann, & D. Reisberg (Eds.), *Perception and mental representation*. New York: Oxford University Press.

Reisberg, D., & Chambers, D. (1991). Neither pictures nor propositions: What can we learn from a mental image? *Canadian Journal of Psychology, 45*, 288–302.

Reisberg, D., & Logie, R.H. (1993). The ins and outs of visual working memory. Overcoming the limits on learning from imagery. In M. Intons-Peterson, B. Roskos-Ewoldsen, & R. Anderson (Eds.), *Imagery, creativity, and discovery: A cognitive approach*, pp.39–76. Amsterdam: Elsevier.

Richardson, J.T.E. (1979). Mental imagery, human memory, and the effects of closed head injury. *British Journal of Social and Clinical Psychology, 18*, 319–327.

Richardson, J.T.E. (1980). *Mental imagery and human memory*. London: Macmillan.

Richardson, J.T.E. (1984). The effects of closed head injury upon intrusions and confusions in free recall. *Cortex, 20*, 413–420.

Richardson, J.T.E. (1987). The role of mental imagery in models of transitive inference. *British Journal of Psychology 78*, 189–203.

Richardson, J.T.E., & Baddeley, A.D. (1975). The effect of articulatory suppression in free recall. *Journal of Verbal Learning and Verbal Behavior, 14,* 623–629.

Richardson, J.T.E., & Barry, C. (1985). The effects of minor closed head injury upon human memory: Further evidence on the role of mental imagery. *Cognitive Neuropsychology, 2,* 149–168.

Riddoch, M.J. (1990). Loss of visual imagery: A generation deficit. *Cognitive Neuropsychology, 7,* 249–273.

Riddoch, M.J., & Humphreys, G.W. (1983). The effect of cueing on unilateral neglect. *Neuropsychologia, 21,* 589–599.

Robin, F., & Denis, M. (1991). Description of perceived or imagined spatial networks. In R.H. Logie & M. Denis (Eds.), *Mental images in human cognition,* pp.141–152. Amsterdam: North Holland Press.

Rondot, P., de Recondo, J., & Ribadeau Dumas, J.L. (1977). Visuomotor ataxia. *Brain, 100,* 355–376.

Ross, E.D. (1980). Sensory-specific and fractional disorders of recent memory in man. I. Isolated loss of visual recent memory. *Archives of Neurology, 37,* 193–200.

Ruchkin, D.S., Johnson, R., Grafman, J., Canoune, H., & Ritter, W. (1992). Distinctions and similarities among working memory processes: An event-related potential study. *Cognitive Brain Research, 1,* 53–66.

Rugg, M.D. (1984). Event-related potentials in phonological matching tasks. *Brain and Language, 23,* 225–240.

Rumelhart, D.E., & McClelland, J.L. (1986). *Parallel distributed processing: explorations in the microstructure of cognition, Vol 1: Foundations.* Cambridge, MA: MIT Press.

Rundus, D. (1971). Analysis of rehearsal processes in free recall. *Journal of Experimental Psychology, 89,* 63–77.

Saariluoma, P. (1991). Visuo-spatial interference and apperception in chess. In R.H. Logie & M. Denis (Eds.), *Mental images in human cognition.* Amsterdam: Elsevier.

Saffran, E.M., & Marin, O.S.M. (1975). Immediate memory for word lists and sentences in a patient with deficient auditory short-term memory. *Brain and Language, 2,* 420–433.

Salamé, P., & Baddeley, A.D. (1982). Disruption of short-term memory by unattended speech: Implications for the structure of working memory. *Journal of Verbal Learning and Verbal Behavior, 21,* 150–164.

Salamé, P., & Baddeley, A.D. (1989). Effects of background music on phonological short-term memory. *Quarterly Journal of Experimental Psychology, 41*A, 107–122.

Salthouse, T.A., Mitchell, D.R., Skovronek, E., & Babcock, R.L. (1989). Effects of adult age and working memory on reasoning and spatial abilities. *Journal of Experimental Psychology: Learning, Memory, and Cognition, 15,* 507–516.

Salway, A.F.S. (1991). *Random generation in the working memory dual-task paradigm.* Unpublished PhD thesis, University of Aberdeen, Scotland, UK.

Schneider, W., & Detweiler, M. (1987). A connectionist/control architecture for working memory. In G.H. Bower (Ed.), *The psychology of learning and motivation,* Vol. 21. New York: Academic Press.

Schreter, Z., & Pfeifer, R. (1989). Short-term memory/long-term memory interactions in connectionist simulations of psychological experiments on list learning. In L. Personnaz & G. Dreyfus (Eds.), *Neural networks: From models to applications*. Paris: Institut pour le Developpement de la Science, de l'Education et de la Technologie (IDSET).

Schweickert, R., & Boruff, B. (1986). Short-term memory capacity: Magic number or magic spell? *Journal of Experimental Psychology: Learning, Memory, and Cognition, 12*, 419–425.

Schweickert, R., Guentert, L., & Hersberger, L. (1989). Neural network models of memory span. In *Proceedings of the eleventh annual conference of the Cognitive Science Society*. Hillsdale, NJ: Lawrence Erlbaum Associates Inc.

Scoville, W.B., & Milner, B. (1957). Loss of recent memory after bilateral hippocampal lesions. *Journal of Neurology, Neurosurgery and Psychiatry, 20*, 11–21.

Sergent, J. (1989). Image generation and processing of generated images in the cerebral hemispheres. *Journal of Experimental Psychology: Human Perception and Performance, 15*, 170–178.

Shallice, T. (1988) *From neuropsychology to mental structure*. Cambridge, UK: Cambridge University Press.

Shallice, T., & Butterworth, B. (1977). Short-term memory impairment and spontaneous speech. *Neuropsychologia, 15*, 729–735.

Shallice, T., & Warrington, E.K. (1970). Independent functioning of verbal memory stores: A neuropsychological study. *Quarterly Journal of Experimental Psychology, 22*, 261–273.

Shepard, R.N., & Cooper, L.A. (1982). *Mental images and their transformations*. Cambridge, MA: MIT Press.

Shepard, R.N., & Metzler, J. (1971). Mental rotation of three-dimensional objects. *Science, 171*, 701–703.

Shimamura, A.P. (1989) Disorders of memory: The cognitive science perspective. In F. Boller & J. Grafman (Eds.), *Handbook of neuropsychology*, Vol. 3, pp. 35–73. Amsterdam: Elsevier.

Shoben, E.D., Cech, C.G., Schwanenflugel, P.J., & Sailor, K.M. (1989). Serial position effects in comparative judgements. *Journal of Experimental Psychology: Human Perception and Performance, 15*, 273–286.

Shulman, H.G. (1970). Encoding and retention of semantic and phonemic information in short-term memory. *Journal of Verbal Learning and Verbal Behavior, 9*, 499–508.

Siegler, R.S. (1987). The perils of averaging data over strategies: An example from children's addition. *Journal of Experimental Psychology: General, 116*, 250–264.

Smith, M.L., & Milner, B. (1989). Right hippocampal impairment in the recall of spatial location: Encoding deficit or rapid forgetting? *Neuropsychologia, 27*, 71–81.

Smyth, M.M., Pearson, N.A., & Pendleton, L.R. (1988). Movement and working memory: Patterns and positions in space. *Quarterly Journal of Experimental Psychology, 40*A, 497–514.

Smyth, M.M., & Pendleton, L.R. (1989). Working memory for movements. *Quarterly Journal of Experimental Psychology, 41*A, 235–250.

Sperling, G. (1960). The information available in brief visual presentations. *Psychological Monographs: General and Applied, 74*, 1–29.

Spinnler, H., & Della Sala, S. (1988). The role of clinical neuropsychology in the neurological diagnosis of Alzheimer's disease. *Journal of Neurology, 235*, 258–271.

Spinnler, H., Della Sala, S., Bandera, R., & Baddeley, A.D. (1988). Dementia and structure of human memory. *Cognitive Neuropsychology, 5*, 193–211.

Stein, J.F. (1992). The representation of egocentric space in the posterior parietal cortex. *Behavioral and Brain Sciences, 15*, 691–700.

Stigler, J.W., Lee, S.Y., & Stevenson, H.W. (1986). Digit memory in Chinese and English: Evidence for a temporally limited store. *Cognition, 24*, 1–20.

Sullivan, E.V., & Sagar, H.J. (1991). Double dissociation of short-term and long-term memory for nonverbal material in Parkinson's disease and global amnesia. *Brain, 114*, 893–906.

Teuber, H-L. (1955). Physiological psychology. *Annual Review of Psychology, 9*, 267–296.

Teuber, H-L, Milner, B., & Vaughan, H.G. (1968). Persistent anterograde amnesia after a stab wound in the basal brain. *Neuropsychologia, 6*, 267–282.

Thomson, J.A. (1986). Intermittent versus continuous visual control: A reply to Elliott. *Journal of Experimental Psychology: Human Perception and Performance, 12*, 392–393.

Tresch, M.C., Sinnamon, H.M., & Seamon, J.G. (1993). Double dissociation of spatial and object visual memory: Evidence from selective interference in intact human subjects. *Neuropsychologia, 31*, 211–219.

Turner, M.L., & Engle, R.W. (1989). Is working memory capacity task dependent? *Journal of Memory and Language, 28*, 127–154.

Tzeng, O.J.L. (1973). Positive recency effects in delayed free recall. *Journal of Verbal Learning and Verbal Behavior, 12*, 436–439.

Ungerleider, L.G., & Mishkin, M. (1982). Two cortical visual systems. In D.J. Ingle, R.J.W. Mansfield, & M.S. Goodale (Eds.), *The analysis of visual behavior*. Cambridge, MA: MIT Press.

Ungerleider, S., & Golding, J.M. (1991). Mental practice among Olympic athletes. *Perceptual and Motor Skills, 72*, 1007–1017.

Vallar, G., & Baddeley, A.D. (1984). Fractionation of working memory: Neuropsychological evidence for a phonological short-term store. *Journal of Verbal Learning and Verbal Behavior, 23*, 151–161.

Vallar, G., & Baddeley, A.D. (1987). Phonological short-term store and sentence processing. *Cognitive Neuropsychology, 4*, 417–438.

Vallar, G., & Papagno C. (1986). Phonological short-term store and the nature of the recency effect: Evidence from neuropsychology. *Brain and Cognition, 5*, 428–442.

Van Essen, D.C., Anderson, C.H., & Felleman, D.J. (1992). Information processing in the primate visual system: An integrated systems perspective. *Science, 255*, 419–423.

van Sommers, P. (1989). A system for drawing and drawing related psychology. *Cognitive Neuropsychology, 6*, 117–164.

Wagenaar, W.A. (1972). Generation of random sequences by human subjects: A critical survey of the literature. *Psychological Bulletin, 77*, 65–72.

Wagner, D. (1978). Memories of Morocco: the influence of age, schooling, and environment on memory. *Cognitive Psychology, 10*, 1–28

Warren, M.W. (1977). The effects of recall-concurrent visual-motor distraction on picture and word recall. *Memory and Cognition, 5*, 362–370.

Warrington, E.K., & James, M. (1967). Disorders of visual perception in patients with localised cerebral lesions. *Neuropsychologia, 5*, 253–266

Warrington, E.K., Logue, V., & Pratt, R.T.C. (1971). The anatomical localization of selective impairment of auditory verbal short-term memory. *Neuropsychologia, 9*, 377–387.

Warrington, E K., & Rabin, P. (1971). Visual span of apprehension in patients with unilateral cerebral lesions. *Quarterly Journal of Experimental Psychology, 23*, 423–431.

Warrington, E.K., & Shallice, T. (1969). The selective impairment of auditory verbal short-term memory. *Brain, 92*, 885–896.

Washburn, M.F. (1916). *Movement and mental imagery*. Boston: Houghton Mifflin.

Waters, G.S., Rochon, E., & Caplan, D. (1992). The role of high-level speech planning in rehearsal: Evidence from patients with apraxia of speech. *Journal of Memory and Language, 31*, 54–73.

Watkins, M.J., & Peynircioglu Z.F. (1983). Three recency effects at the same time. *Journal of Verbal Learning and Verbal Behavior, 22*, 375–384.

Watkins, M.J., Peynircioglu, Z.F., & Brems, D.J. (1984). Pictorial rehearsal. *Memory and Cognition, 12*, 553–557.

Waugh, N.C., & Norman, D.A. (1965) Primary memory. *Psychological Review, 72*, 89–104.

Wetherick, N.E. (1975). The role of semantic information in short-term memory. *Journal of Verbal Learning and Verbal Behavior, 14*, 471–480.

Widaman, K.F., Geary, D.C., Cormier, O., & Little, T.D. (1989). A componential model of mental addition. *Journal of Experimental Psychology: Learning, Memory and Cognition, 15*, 898–919.

Wilson, B., & Baddeley, A.D. (1988). Frontal amnesia and the dysexecutive syndrome. *Brain and Cognition, 7*, 212–230.

Wilson, J.T.L., Scott, J.H., & Power, K.G. (1987). Developmental differences in the span of visual memory for pattern. *British Journal of Developmental Psychology, 5*, 249–255.

Wilson, R.S., Bacon, L.D., Fox, J.H., & Kaszniak A.W. (1983). Primary and secondary memory in dementia of the Alzheimer's type. *Journal of Clinical Neuropsychology, 5*, 337–344.

Wolford, G., & Hollingsworth, S. (1974). Evidence that short-term memory is not the limiting factor in tachistoscopic full-report procedure. *Memory and Cognition, 2*, 796–800.

Woodworth, R.S., & Schlosberg, H. (1954). *Experimental psychology*. London: Methuen & Co.

Yuille, J.C., & Paivio, A. (1969). Abstractness and the recall of connected discourse. *Journal of Experimental Psychology, 82*, 467–471.

Zeki, S., & Shipp, S. (1988). The functional logic of cortical connections. *Nature, 335*, 311–317.

Zola-Morgan, S., Squire, L.R., & Ammaral, D.G. (1986). Human amnesia and the medial-temporal region: Enduring memory impairment following a bilateral lesion limited to field CA1 of the hippocampus. *Journal of Neuroscience, 6*, 2950–2967.

Author Index

Subject Index